Contents

THE THEATRE IN SHAKESPEARE'S DAY

On the face of it, the conditions in the Elizabethan theatre were not such as to encourage great writers. The public playhouse itself was not very different from an ordinary inn-yard; it was open to the weather; among the spectators there were often louts, pickpockets and prostitutes; some of the actors played up to the rowdy elements in the audience by inserting their own jokes into the authors' lines, while others spoke their words loudly but unfeelingly; the presentation was often rough and noisy, with fireworks to represent storms and battles, and a table and a few chairs to represent a tavern; there were no actresses, so boys took the parts of women, even such subtle and mature ones as Cleopatra and Lady Macbeth; there was rarely any scenery at all in the modern sense. In fact, a quick inspection of the English theatre in the reign of Elizabeth I by a time-traveller from the twentieth century might well produce only one positive reaction: the costumes were often elaborate and beautiful.

Shakespeare himself makes frequent comments in his plays about the limitations of the playhouse and the actors of his time, often apologizing for them. At the beginning of *Henry V* the Prologue refers to the stage as 'this unworthy scaffold' and to the theatre building (the Globe, probably) as 'this wooden O', and emphasizes the urgent need for imagination in making up for all the deficiencies of presentation. In introducing Act IV the Chorus goes so far as to say:

> '. . . we shall much disgrace
> With four or five most vile and ragged foils,
> Right ill-dispos'd in brawl ridiculous,
> The name of Agincourt.'   (lines 49–52)

In *A Midsummer Night's Dream* (Act V, Scene i) he seems to dismiss actors with the words:

> 'The best in this kind are but shadows.'

4

Yet Elizabeth's theatre, with all its faults, stimulated dramatists to a variety of achievement that has never been equalled and, in Shakespeare, produced one of the greatest writers in history. In spite of all his grumbles he seems to have been fascinated by the challenge that it presented him with. It is necessary to re-examine his theatre carefully in order to understand how he was able to achieve so much with the materials he chose to use. What sort of place was the Elizabethan playhouse in reality? What sort of people were these criticized actors? And what sort of audiences gave them their living?

The Development of the Theatre up to Shakespeare's Time

For centuries in England noblemen had employed groups of skilled people to entertain them when required. Under Tudor rule, as England became more secure and united, actors such as these were given more freedom, and they often performed in public, while still acknowledging their 'overlords' (in the 1570s, for example, when Shakespeare was still a schoolboy at Stratford, one famous company was called 'Lord Leicester's Men'). London was rapidly becoming larger and more important in the second half of the sixteenth century, and many of the companies of actors took the opportunities offered to establish themselves at inns on the main roads leading to the City (for example, the Boar's Head in Whitechapel and the Tabard in Southwark) or in the City itself. These groups of actors would come to an agreement with the inn-keeper which would give them the use of the yard for their performances after people had eaten and drunk well in the middle of the day. Before long, some inns were taken over completely by companies of players and thus became the first public theatres. In 1574 the officials of the City of London issued an order which shows clearly that these theatres were both popular and also offensive to some respectable people, because the order complains about 'the inordinate haunting of great multitudes of people, specially youth, to plays, interludes and shows; namely occasion of frays and quarrels, evil practices of incontinency in great inns . . .' There is evidence that, on public holidays, the theatres on the banks of the Thames were crowded with noisy apprentices and tradesmen, but it would be wrong to think that audiences were always undiscriminating and loud-mouthed. In spite of the disapproval of Puritans and the more staid members of society, by the 1590s, when Shakespeare's plays were beginning to be performed, audiences consisted of a good cross-section of English society, nobility as well as workers, intellectuals as well as simple people out for a laugh; also (and in this respect English theatres were unique in Europe), it was quite normal for respectable women to attend plays. So Shakespeare had to write plays which would appeal to people of widely different kinds. He had to provide 'something for everyone' but at the same time to take care to unify the material so that it would not seem to fall into separate pieces as they watched it. A speech like that of the drunken porter in *Macbeth* could provide the 'groundlings' with a belly-laugh, but also held a deeper significance for those who could appreciate it. The audience he wrote for was one of a number of apparent drawbacks which Shakespeare was able to turn to his and our advantage.

Shakespeare's Actors

Nor were all the actors of the time mere 'rogues, vagabonds and sturdy beggars' as some were described in a Statute of 1572. It is true that many of them had a hard life and earned very little money, but leading actors could become partners in the ownership of the theatres in which they acted: Shakespeare was a shareholder in the Globe and the Blackfriars theatres when he was an actor as well as a playwright. In any case, the attacks made on Elizabethan actors were usually directed at their morals and not at their acting ability; it is clear that many of them must have been good at their trade if they were able to interpret complex works like the great tragedies in such a way as to attract enthusiastic audiences. Undoubtedly some of the boys took the women's parts with skill and confidence, since a man called Coryate, visiting Venice in 1611, expressed surprise that women could act as well as they: 'I saw women act, a thing that I never saw before . . . and they performed it with as good a grace, action, gesture . . . as ever I saw any masculine actor.' The quality of most of the actors who first presented Shakespeare's plays is probably accurately summed up by Fynes Moryson, who wrote, '. . . as there be, in my opinion, more plays in London than in all the parts of the world I have seen, so do these players or comedians excel all other in the world.'

The Structure of the Public Theatre

Although the 'purpose-built' theatres were based on the inn-yards which had been used for play-acting, most of them were circular. The walls contained galleries on three storeys from which the wealthier patrons watched; they must have been something like the 'boxes' in a modern theatre, except that they held much larger numbers – as many as 1500. The 'groundlings' stood on the floor of the building, facing a raised stage which projected from the 'stage-wall', the main features of which were:

1. a small room opening on to the back of the main stage and on the same level as it (rear stage);
2. a gallery above this inner stage (upper stage);
3. a canopy projecting from above the gallery over the main stage, to protect the actors from the weather (the 700 or 800 members of the audience who occupied the yard, or 'pit' as we call it today, had the sky above them).

In addition to these features there were dressing-rooms behind the stage and a space underneath it from which entrances could be made through trap-doors. All the acting areas – main stage, rear stage, upper stage and under stage – could be entered by actors directly from their dressing-rooms, and all of them were used in productions of Shakespeare's plays. For example, the inner stage, an almost cave-like structure, would have been where Ferdinand and Miranda are 'discovered' playing chess in the last act of *The Tempest*, while the upper stage was certainly the balcony

7

from which Romeo climbs down in Act III of *Romeo and Juliet.*

It can be seen that such a building, simple but adaptable, was not really unsuited to the presentation of plays like Shakespeare's. On the contrary, its simplicity guaranteed the minimum of distraction, while its shape and construction must have produced a sense of involvement on the part of the audience that modern producers would envy.

Other Resources of the Elizabethan Theatre

Although there were few attempts at scenery in the public theatre (painted backcloths were occasionally used in court performances), Shakespeare and his fellow playwrights were able to make use of a fair variety of 'properties'; lists of such articles have survived: they include beds, tables, thrones, and also trees, walls, a gallows, a Trojan horse and a 'Mouth of Hell'; in a list of properties belonging to the manager, Philip Henslowe, the curious item 'two mossy banks' appears. Possibly one of them was used for the

'bank whereon the wild thyme blows,
Where ox-lips and the nodding violet grows'

in *A Midsummer Night's Dream* (Act II, Scene i). Once again, imagination must have been required of the audience.

Costumes were the one aspect of stage production in which trouble and expense were hardly ever spared to obtain a magnificent effect. Only occasionally did they attempt any historical accuracy (almost all Elizabethan productions were what we should call 'modern-dress' ones), but they were appropriate to the characters who wore them: kings were seen to be kings and beggars were similarly unmistakable. It is an odd fact that there was usually no attempt at illusion in the costuming: if a costume *looked* fine and rich it probably *was*. Indeed, some of the costumes were almost unbelievably expensive. Henslowe lent his company £19 to buy a cloak, and the Alleyn brothers, well-known actors, gave £20 for a 'black velvet cloak, with sleeves embroidered all with silver and gold, lined with black satin striped with gold'.

SHAKESPEARE'S LIFE AND TIMES

Very little indeed is known about Shakespeare's private life: the facts included here are almost the only indisputable ones. The dates of Shakespeare's plays are those on which they were first produced.

* * *

1558 Queen Elizabeth crowned.
1561 Francis Bacon born.
1564 Christopher Marlowe born. William Shakespeare born, April 23rd, baptized April 26th.
1566 Shakespeare's brother, Gilbert, born.
1567 Mary, Queen of Scots, deposed.
James VI (later James I of England) crowned King of Scotland.
1572 Ben Jonson born.
Lord Leicester's Company (of players) licensed; later called Lord Strange's, then the Lord Chamberlain's, and finally (under James) The King's Men.
1573 John Donne born.
1574 The Common Council of London directs that all plays and playhouses in London must be licensed.
1576 James Burbage builds the first public playhouse, The Theatre, at Shoreditch, outside the walls of the City.
1577 Francis Drake begins his voyage round the world (completed 1580).
Holinshed's *Chronicles of England, Scotland and Ireland* published (which Shakespeare later used extensively).
1582 Shakespeare married to Anne Hathaway.

9

1583 The Queen's Company founded by royal warrant.	Shakespeare's daughter, Susanna, born.
1585	Shakespeare's twins, Hamnet and Judith, born.
1586 Sir Philip Sidney, the Elizabethan ideal 'Christian knight', poet, patron, soldier, killed at Zutphen in the Low Countries.	
1587 Mary, Queen of Scots, beheaded. Marlowe's *Tamburlaine* (*Part I*) first staged.	
1588 Defeat of the Spanish Armada. Marlowe's *Tamburlaine* (*Part II*) first staged.	
1589 Marlowe's *Jew of Malta* and Kyd's *Spanish Tragedy* (a 'revenge tragedy' and one of the most popular plays of Elizabethan times).	
1590 Spenser's *Faerie Queene* (Books I-III) published.	
1592 Marlowe's *Doctor Faustus* and *Edward II* first staged. Witchcraft trials in Scotland. Robert Greene, a rival playwright, refers to Shakespeare as 'an upstart crow' and 'the only Shake-scene in a country'.	*Titus Andronicus* *Henry VI, Parts I, II and III* *Richard III*
1593 London theatres closed by the plague. Christopher Marlowe killed in a Deptford tavern.	*Two Gentlemen of Verona* *Comedy of Errors* *The Taming of the Shrew* *Love's Labour's Lost*
1594 Shakespeare's company becomes The Lord Chamberlain's Men.	*Romeo and Juliet*
1595 Raleigh's first expedition to Guiana. Last expedition of Drake and Hawkins (both died).	*Richard II* *A Midsummer Night's Dream*

1596 Spenser's *Faerie Queene* (Books IV-VI) published. James Burbage buys rooms at Blackfriars and begins to convert them into a theatre.

King John
The Merchant of Venice
Shakespeare's son Hamnet dies. Shakespeare's father is granted a coat of arms.

1597 James Burbage dies; his son Richard, a famous actor, turns the Blackfriars Theatre into a private playhouse.

Henry IV (Part I)
Shakespeare buys and redecorates New Place at Stratford.

1598 Death of Philip II of Spain.

Henry IV (Part II)
Much Ado About Nothing

1599 Death of Edmund Spenser. The Globe Theatre completed at Bankside by Richard and Cuthbert Burbage.

Henry V
Julius Caesar
As You Like It

1600 Fortune Theatre built at Cripplegate. East India Company founded for the extension of English trade and influence in the East. The Children of the Chapel begin to use the hall at Blackfriars.

Merry Wives of Windsor
Troilus and Cressida

1601

Hamlet
Twelfth Night

1602 Sir Thomas Bodley's library opened at Oxford.

1603 Death of Queen Elizabeth. James I comes to the throne. Shakespeare's company becomes The King's Men. Raleigh tried, condemned and sent to the Tower.

1604 Treaty of peace with Spain.

Measure for Measure
Othello
All's Well that Ends Well

1605 The Gunpowder Plot: an attempt by a group of Catholics to blow up the Houses of Parliament.

1606 Guy Fawkes and other plotters executed.

Macbeth
King Lear

11

1607 Virginia, in America, colonized.
A great frost in England.

Antony and Cleopatra
Timon of Athens
Coriolanus
Shakespeare's daughter, Susanna, married to Dr. John Hall.

1608 The company of the Children of the Chapel Royal (who had performed at Blackfriars for ten years) is disbanded.
John Milton born.
Notorious pirates executed in London.

Richard Burbage leases the Blackfriars Theatre to six of his fellow actors, including Shakespeare.
Pericles, Prince of Tyre

1609

Shakespeare's *Sonnets* published.

1610 A great drought in England.

Cymbeline

1611 Chapman completes his great translation of the *Iliad*, the story of Troy.
Authorized Version of the Bible published.

A Winter's Tale
The Tempest

1612 Webster's *The White Devil* first staged.

Shakespeare's brother, Gilbert, dies.

1613 Globe Theatre burnt down during a performance of *Henry VIII* (the firing of small cannon set fire to the thatched roof).
Webster's *Duchess of Malfi* first staged.

Henry VIII
Two Noble Kinsmen
Shakespeare buys a house at Blackfriars.

1614 Globe Theatre rebuilt 'in far finer manner than before'.

1616 Ben Jonson publishes his plays in one volume.
Raleigh released from the Tower in order to prepare an expedition to the gold mines of Guiana.

Shakespeare's daughter, Judith, marries Thomas Quiney.
Death of Shakespeare on his birthday, April 23rd.

1618 Raleigh returns to England and is executed on the charge for which he was imprisoned in 1603.

1623 Publication of the Folio edition of Shakespeare's plays.

Death of Anne Shakespeare (née Hathaway).

INTRODUCTION

Julius Caesar is a play which readily appeals to modern audiences. In fact, it must surely be one of the plays that have helped persuade a modern critic to describe Shakespeare as our 'contemporary'.

The subject matter of the play is probably one reason for this, for it is largely concerned with violence as a means of achieving social justice. Whether the freedom from oppression justifies what we now call terrorism is a pressing contemporary issue, as is the study of past and present dictators. *Julius Caesar* should not be seen as a political exposition, however. Neither the political nor the historical framework of the play is Shakespeare's main concern: they simply provide him with an opportunity to explore the complex motives and personalities of the characters in the play, and other themes which transcend these characters.

One such theme is the part played by fate in people's lives – can we control our own destinies, or must we submit to a pre-ordained pattern of events? Calphurnia's warning dream and the omens described before Caesar's murder increase the dramatic tension within the play, and make the audience or reader feel that events are moving inexorably on, on a heavenly as well as a human scale. As Caesar himself says:

> *Of all the wonders that I yet have heard,*
> *It seems to me most strange that men should fear,*
> *Seeing that death, a necessary end,*
> *Will come when it will come.*
>
> (Act II, Scene ii, lines 34–7)

The theme of death is closely related to that of fate, as we are frequently reminded of the ultimate doom that awaits us all. We are also made aware of the way in which Caesar's spirit is present in the play after his murder has been effected. The conspirators may have killed Caesar, but they cannot destroy his presence.

13

The Language of the Play

Although much has been written about Shakespeare's skill with language, it is easy to forget that he was first and foremost a poet. Few plays today are written in verse and, with the emphasis on other elements such as psychological study, modern audiences are not as aware of, or able to appreciate, poetic qualities. So it is right to call attention to Shakespeare's poetry.

Nevertheless, it is probably true to say that *Julius Caesar* has fewer essentially poetic characteristics than other plays by Shakespeare. This does not mean that the language is not eloquent and forceful, but its eloquence stems from thought, observation or argumentative skill rather than vivid imagination alone. A marked exception is the well-known speech by Brutus near the end of the play:

> *There is a tide in the affairs of men*
> *Which, taken at the flood, leads on to fortune ...*
>
> (Act IV, Scene iii, lines 220–1)

But an equally well-known speech by Caesar makes an interesting comparison:

> *Would he were fatter! But I fear him not.*
> *Yet, if my name were liable to fear,*
> *I do not know the man I should avoid*
> *So soon as that spare Cassius.*
>
> (Act I, Scene ii, lines 199–202)

Caesar goes on to say that Cassius has no love of entertainment, smiles in a cynical way and is never content when in the presence of somebody more powerful than himself.

Such a speech gives a remarkably penetrating insight into Cassius's character, but an interesting fact is that it contains hardly any imagery at all, and what there is is not very striking. This is in contrast to many of the great speeches from Shakespeare's plays in which powerful emotions are expressed by means of vivid similes and metaphors. It would be misleading to say that Caesar's speech is typical of the play, but it does indicate that the language of *Julius Caesar* has its own quite striking qualities. Caesar's remarks are those of a suspicious man, fearful for his own safety. They form a brilliant description of Cassius, but at the same

14

time reveal Caesar himself in all his uneasiness and lack of self-awareness, masked by a superficial self-confidence and assertiveness.

Much of the language of this play is of a rhetorical, argumentative or persuasive kind, because much of the play consists of people trying to change the attitudes and thoughts of others. The best examples of this are Antony's great forum speeches, which are brilliant in their use of irony, suggestion and the power of shocking the Roman people into action:—

> This was the most unkindest cut of all;
> For when the noble Caesar saw him stab,
> Ingratitude, more strong than traitors' arms,
> Quite vanquish'd him. Then burst his mighty heart;
> And in his mantle muffling up his face,
> Even at the base of Pompey's statua,
> Which all the while ran blood, great Caesar fell.
>
> (Act III, Scene ii, lines 185–91)

Similarly, the quarrel between Brutus and Cassius (Act IV, Scene iii) with its uninhibited expression of anger, indignation and pain, depends for its effect upon the tension of the relationship between the two men. Only on rare occasions do characters calmly reflect and soliloquize.

Characterization

The practice of studying and assessing characters in Shakespeare's plays no longer plays such a dominant part in the criticism that continues to be written about them. This is not surprising, since each generation must find its own way to their essential quality and value. Nevertheless, *Julius Caesar* does seem, more than most of the plays, to lend itself to a study of the people in it. The whole sweep of the drama depends upon the fears, desires or ambitions of individuals, or just the evident defects of their personalities. Of all Shakespeare's plays, this one is a good example of 'character in action'.

Caesar and Brutus are studied in detail in the 'Summing Up', page 226, so let us now look at Cassius. His restless, gnawing resentment is plain in the speeches in Act I where he tries to persuade Brutus to lead a conspiracy, and reveals far more about himself than Caesar. Cassius seems to be a man driven on relentlessly by his own hatred, the strength of which can be seen by the number of occasions on which he talks of his own death as preferable to a life encumbered by the kind of danger or suffering that he has to endure, whether it be the tyranny of Caesar, the hostility of Brutus or the realization that he has sent one of his own officers to his death. And yet Cassius, lacking Brutus's idealism, has a better grasp of the practicalities of a murderous conspiracy. In particular, he *looks/Quite through the deeds of men* (Act I, Scene ii, lines 203–4), especially Antony whom he deeply mistrusts, and events prove him to be right. He is not lacking in warmth and sensitivity and is deeply hurt when Brutus accuses him of betraying their cause. Yet, we cannot forget the trick Cassius played on Brutus with the forged letters, nor his willingness to condone bribery. Just as it is difficult to discover whether there is a hero in this play and, if so, who it is, in the same way it would be a mistake to identify Cassius as the villain.

Can we identify Antony as the villain of the play? The clever way in which he deceives the conspirators, his eager participation in the purging of his enemies, his cunning manipulation of the crowd and (as it seems) his attempt to deprive the people of Rome of some of the benefits of Caesar's will, all suggest that he is. Yet this eloquent and ambitious man is partly redeemed by his love of Caesar. That this love is genuine can be seen not in his flattering comment, *When Caesar says 'Do this', it is perform'd* (Act I, Scene ii, line 11), but much more forcefully in his heartfelt speech of sorrow over the body of Caesar (Act III, Scene i, lines 255–76); and this speech is made in the presence of the murderers whose friendship he needs to cultivate. He is so overcome that he has to be brought back to the immediate situation by Cassius asking him what his intentions are. Antony *is* shrewd and devious, both before and after this incident, but that does not alter the sincerity of his feelings. It is not altogether surprising, therefore, if this passionate sincerity is expressed in his funeral oration, in which he seems to be inspired and elevated in a way that would not have seemed possible from what we know of him at this stage. However crafty and unjust he may be to the conspirators, we cannot fail to be carried away by the breathtaking audacity and power of what he says here. It is a triumph of emotion and imagination over reason (the 'reason' of Brutus), and the impetus for such a speech springs from Antony's love for Caesar.

Thus, the instinctive desire of many audiences and readers for neat, black-and-white characters is never satisfied in this play. Some readers may see more or less good in any of the characters that have been described here, but simple generalizations would not do them justice. So it is with some of the minor characters, especially Casca. In Act I, Scene ii – in which he describes the attempted crowning of Caesar – he is little more than a buffoon, sneering at the crowd and Caesar, and seeming to be disinclined even to talk about what had happened. But he is also described as having once been 'quick mettle' (Act I, Scene ii, line 297) and is, in fact, the first to strike Caesar. In the storm, oddly enough, he is terrified by the strange signs which have to be interpreted for him by Cassius.

One final point needs to be made about the women of this play. Both of them are very obviously presented as subordinate to their husbands, but in different ways. Calphurnia is treated patronizingly by Caesar, as if she were a child and he fairly readily contradicts her by changing his mind about going to the Senate. He also humiliates her by referring to her 'sterile curse' in public (Act I, Scene ii, line 9). In marked contrast, Portia is treated with grave courtesy and affection by Brutus when she begs him to tell her what is going on. One feels that they have a real relationship within the bond of marriage whereas Caesar and Calphurnia do not.

Plot

Act I   Caesar has recently won a battle and the people of Rome are turning out to celebrate his victory in a Triumph (special victory procession). The Tribunes of the people are angry because Caesar had not defeated any enemy of Rome but simply another Roman, one of the sons of Pompey, and Pompey had enjoyed the support of the people. The Tribunes disperse the people and do their best, by removing all the signs of festivity, to take the heart out of the celebrations.

Caesar appears briefly at the games that celebrate the feast of Lupercal. He wants Antony to touch Calphurnia because he feels it will remove her 'sterile curse', and he dismisses the soothsayer's warning about the Ides of March. When he has moved away, Cassius attempts to sound out Brutus's attitude to Caesar by cross-questioning him closely. He describes incidents in Caesar's earlier life when he appeared to be merely human – even hopelessly weak – to show how this ordinary man has now become a god in the eyes of the people. He talks bitterly about the power Caesar wields and how Rome has lost its soul to allow such a man to gain supreme power. Brutus is sympathetic but will not commit himself.

The returning Caesar makes some suspicious but shrewd comments about Cassius. After he has left, Casca makes some equally shrewd comments about Caesar, reporting how he had, with some reluctance, rejected a crown offered to him three times by Antony. Finally, Cassius, when alone, cynically observes how easily he feels he can sway Brutus into leading a conspiracy against Caesar.

In Scene iii, there is a violent storm that frightens Casca but encourages Cassius, who takes the thunder and lightning and other strange events as signs that the gods want to warn Romans of coming disaster. He clearly believes that it is Caesar that they are displeased with. He urges Casca and Cinna to join the conspiracy he has started, which they seem willing to do. But they all know that success depends upon whether they can persuade one man to lead them – Brutus.

Act II Alone at his home, Brutus struggles with his conscience about the plan to murder Caesar. Some messages have been thrown in through his window (forged by Cassius), which convince him that the people of Rome long for him to stand up for them. By the time the party of conspirators arrives, Brutus has made up his mind to join them.

The details of the plot are discussed and at once Brutus stamps his authority on his fellow conspirators by rejecting some of their suggestions. He will not allow an oath to be taken, believing that they are all honourable Romans. Secondly, he refuses to allow Cicero into the plot. Most important of all, he will not allow Antony, a known friend of Caesar, to be killed as well. Such an act, he thinks, would turn their plot from a kind of sacrifice into mere butchery. The plan is for them all to call on Caesar in the morning to escort him to the Capitol. The conspirators leave and Brutus promises to tell his worried wife all about the reasons for his sleeplessness and anxiety.

In the latter part of this Act, at Caesar's house, Calphurnia begs her husband not to attend the Capitol because of the storm that is raging and a dream she has had in which Caesar's statue spouted blood. Decius quickly puts a more favourable interpretation on this dream and thus persuades Caesar to change his mind. Tension is increased by a minor character, Artemidorus, who has obviously got wind of the plot and wants to warn Caesar, and by the Soothsayer's ambiguous remarks to Portia.

Act III At the Capitol, where Caesar is to deal with requests and petitions, Metellus Cimber begs to have his brother recalled from banishment. The request is harshly refused and the conspirators all begin to stab Caesar. Caesar survives until his friend Brutus stabs him and then surrenders his life in amazement. The murderers are exultant, believing that they can carry the people of Rome with them, but they have not reckoned with Antony. After shrewdly gaining assurances of safe conduct, he arrives to deplore the spectacle of Caesar's mangled body. In a dramatic gesture, he invites the conspirators to kill him as well since he would regard it as an honour to die in the same hour as Caesar and at the hands of the same assassins. Brutus is touched by his apparent sincerity but Cassius wants to know where Antony stands; is he for them or against them? Antony declares himself on their side and asks for leave to give Caesar's funeral oration – an honour usually given to the dead man's closest friend. In spite of Cassius's objections, Brutus agrees. Left alone, Antony reveals his true intentions – to gain his revenge for Caesar's death, no matter what the cost.

Then follows the great forum scene, in which an angry and restless crowd is at first convinced by the sincere, but cool and rational, arguments of Brutus that it was necessary for Caesar to be killed for the good of Rome. According to Brutus, Caesar had many virtues for which credit should be given, but he was also ambitious and, for that, death is the proper punishment.

Antony follows with his speech and cunningly begins by dwelling on the accepted greatness of Caesar and the benefits he had brought to Rome. Doubts are raised in the crowd's mind; he repeatedly describes the conspirators as 'honourable' until it is apparent the word is plainly sarcastic. He hints that there are many generous gifts for the people in Caesar's will, which he has but does not intend to read, thus creating a demand for it to be read. The passions of the people are roused by his uncovering the body of Caesar, and Antony finally inflames them to such an extent that they riot through the streets of Rome and drive out the conspirators.

With Caesar dead and the conspirators driven away, Rome is governed by a Triumvirate consisting of Antony, Octavius Caesar and Lepidus. We see at once that Rome has fallen out of the frying pan into the fire for these men, entirely lacking the honourable qualities of Brutus, are

20

engaged in the process of ruthless extermination of their enemies, even including some who are their own relatives. The three men are also clearly not on good terms with one another.

The scene then shifts from Rome to Brutus' camp, where he is awaiting the arrival of Cassius. These two also have their differences and, when Cassius arrives, there is a bitter quarrel between them. The subject of this is essentially the question of whether it is possible to succeed in their aims while retaining the ideals and principles of justice that Brutus originally insisted upon. Eventually, they make it up and Cassius realizes that one reason for his friend's bad temper was the death of his wife, Portia.

The two of them, with their officers, then plan their campaign. Are they to march directly against the forces of Antony and Octavius or remain where they are? Cassius says they should stay where they are, compelling the enemy to tire and waste resources searching for them. Brutus prefers to move, arguing, in a persuasive speech, that 'there is a tide in the affairs of men' and that the tide is flowing their way but will not last. Once again, Brutus has his way, but later that night he is dismayed by the appearance of the ghost of Caesar, who says they will meet at Philippi.

Act V   Before the battle, the rival leaders meet for a parley. There is little chance of a peaceful outcome since both sides seem to prefer to justify themselves and abuse their opponents. Just before battle begins, Cassius seems oppressed by a deep sense of foreboding and he and Brutus discuss their respective philosophies, both of them apparently beginning to doubt the beliefs that had sustained them during their lives.

The battle is confusing and Brutus, according to one account, attacks too soon and then allows his troops to waste time on plunder after gaining an initial advantage. In his depressed state of mind,

Cassius thinks that some friendly troops are hostile and persuades his bondman to stab him. Brutus speaks in glowing terms of his dead friend and is sustained for a time by the great loyalty of his followers. But it is clear that his cause is lost, especially when he reveals that the ghost of Caesar has appeared to him a second time. He runs on to his sword. The play ends as Antony and Octavius acknowledge the nobility of the man who had murdered Caesar so reluctantly.

This summary of the plot shows that there are no real 'winners' in this play. The three main characters who die – Caesar, Cassius and Brutus – all leave us with a sense of loss, in spite of their faults or errors. All of them, in fact, are the subject of admiring and even passionate speeches of regret after their deaths. Antony and Octavius remain, but Antony, though a powerful and colourful character, has lost most of our sympathy because of his deviousness and ruthlessness. Octavius's character is only slightly developed but it is clear that these two are unlikely to form a harmonious partnership for the benefit of Rome.

LIST OF CHARACTERS

JULIUS CAESAR

OCTAVIUS CAESAR
MARCUS ANTONIUS
M. AEMIL. LEPIDUS
} *Triumvirs after the death of Julius Caesar*

CICERO
PUBLIUS
POPILIUS LENA
} *senators*

MARCUS BRUTUS
CASSIUS
CASCA
TREBONIUS
LIGARIUS
DECIUS BRUTUS
METELLUS CIMBER
CINNA
} *conspirators against Julius Caesar*

FLAVIUS *and* MARULLUS *tribunes*
ARTEMIDORUS, *a sophist of Cnidos*
A SOOTHSAYER
CINNA, *a poet*
ANOTHER POET

LUCILIUS
TITINIUS
MESSALA
YOUNG CATO
VOLUMNIUS
} *friends to Brutus and Cassius*

VARRO
CLITUS
CLAUDIUS
STRATO
LUCIUS
DARDANIUS
} *servants to Brutus*

PINDARUS, *servant to Cassius*
CALPHURNIA, *wife to Caesar*
PORTIA, *wife to Brutus*
SENATORS, CITIZENS, GUARDS, ATTENDANTS, &C.

THE SCENE: *Rome; near Sardis; near Philippi*

23

NOTES

ACT ONE   SCENE I

Like many of Shakespeare's plays, *Julius Caesar* begins with a dramatic, outdoor crowd scene. It shows us none of the chief characters but is important. One purpose of the scene is to show that Caesar is popular with the common people of Rome, especially because he has won a victory and is about to return in triumph. But this popularity shows that the people have short memories and there are obviously some men in Rome who hate Caesar and think he is gaining too much power. Thus, a sense of tension and conflict is created at once.

3. *mechanical:* artisans; members of the working class. Flavius means that they ought to be at their work; if they were, they would be wearing their working clothes.

8. *apparel:* clothes.

10-11. *in respect of . . . cobbler:*‘ in comparison with a skilled workman I am no more than a bungler’ (A clumsy, incompetent workman is the other meaning of the word ‘cobbler’ which usually means shoe-repairer.)
12. Marullus asks for a simple reply, being irritated by the cobbler's attempt to be witty when he uses the word ‘cobbler’ in this double sense.

14. There is a pun here on the word ‘souls’ (soles of shoes), helped out by the word ‘conscience’.

17. *out:* ‘angry’ and ‘with holes in his shoes’.

ACT ONE

SCENE I—*Rome. A street*

Enter FLAVIUS, MARULLUS, *and certain* COMMONERS
over the stage

Flavius

    Hence! home, you idle creatures, get you home.
    Is this a holiday? What! know you not,
    Being mechanical, you ought not walk
    Upon a labouring day without the sign
    Of your profession? Speak, what trade art thou?   *5*

First Citizen

    Why, sir, a carpenter.

Marullus

    Where is thy leather apron and thy rule?
    What dost thou with thy best apparel on?
    You, sir, what trade are you?

Second Citizen

    Truly, sir, in respect of a fine workman, I am but,   *10*
    as you would say, a cobbler.

Marullus

    But what trade art thou? Answer me directly.

Second Citizen

    A trade, sir, that I hope I may use with a safe con-
    science, which is indeed, sir, a mender of bad soles.

Marullus

    What trade, thou knave? Thou naughty knave,   *15*
    what trade?

Second Citizen

    Nay, I beseech you, sir, be not out with me; yet, if
    you be out, sir, I can mend you.

19-20. Marullus probably understands perfectly well; he is becoming angry at the man's insolence.

23. Note the obvious puns on 'all' and 'awl'. An awl is a tool for making holes in e.g. leather.

26. *re-cover:* 'cure' and 're-sole'.
26-8. *As proper . . . handiwork:* 'As fine men as have ever worn shoes have used my products'.
neat's leather: leather made from the hides of cattle.

32. After this silly comment, there is a clear change in the tone of the language. The serious business of the play has begun.
33. *triumph:* in Roman times, a special procession to celebrate victory, in which captives and plunder were paraded.

35. *tributaries:* captives forced to pay tribute (money).

36. *captive bonds:* prisoners' chains.

37. This contemptuous view of the crowd should be compared with Antony's, shown in Act III, Scene ii, line 142.

39. *Pompey.* Caesar had defeated the *sons* of Pompey who had himself been a popular figure. As the Pompey family were themselves Romans, Caesar was not really entitled to a triumph, according to Roman custom, but Marullus is chiefly shocked by the ingratitude of the people who had originally followed and admired the very man whose sons Caesar had just defeated.
43. *livelong day:* whole day long.

Marullus

What mean'st thou by that? Mend me, thou saucy
fellow! 20

Second Citizen

Why, sir, cobble you.

Flavius

Thou art a cobbler, art thou?

Second Citizen

Truly, sir, all that I live by is with the awl. I meddle
with no tradesman's matters nor women's matters,
but with awl. I am indeed, sir, a surgeon to old shoes. 25
When they are in great danger, I re-cover them. As
proper men as ever trod upon neat's leather have
gone upon my handiwork.

Flavius

But wherefore art not in thy shop to-day?
Why dost thou lead these men about the streets? 30

Second Citizen

Truly, sir, to wear out their shoes, to get myself into
more work. But indeed, sir, we make holiday to see
Caesar, and to rejoice in his triumph.

Marullus

Wherefore rejoice? What conquest brings he home?
What tributaries follow him to Rome, 35
To grace in captive bonds his chariot wheels?
You blocks, you stones, you worse than senseless
    things!
O you hard hearts, you cruel men of Rome,
Knew you not Pompey? Many a time and oft
Have you climb'd up to walls and battlements, 40
To tow'rs and windows, yea, to chimney-tops,
Your infants in your arms, and there have sat
The livelong day, with patient expectation,
To see great Pompey pass the streets of Rome.
And when you saw his chariot but appear, 45
Have you not made an universal shout,
That Tiber trembled underneath her banks,

48. *replication:* echo.

49. *concave shores:* hollowed-out banks.

51. *cull out:* pick out, select.

53. *Pompey's blood:* the sons of Pompey.

56-7. *intermit . . . ingratitude:* 'refrain from inflicting the punishment that must inevitably fall upon this ingratitude.'

59. *sort:* class, group.

60-2. Flavius's rather imaginative idea is that the crowd ought to shed so many tears into the Tiber because of their error and ingratitude, that the river would rise from its lowest level to touch the top of its highest banks.

63. *whe'r:* whether.
basest metal: mean disposition, despicable nature.

66-7. *Disrobe . . . ceremonies:* 'Strip the busts and statues (of Caesar) of their ornaments, if they have been decorated in his honour.'

69. *the feast of Lupercal:* one of the chief Roman festivals, originally in honour of shepherds and herdsmen and associated with the founding of Rome. Obviously, it would be dangerous to show hostility to Caesar at such a time.

71. *trophies:* ornaments in honour of Caesar.

72. *vulgar:* common people.

74. Flavius concludes the scene with a figure of speech comparing Caesar with a hawk (a bird of prey) that likes to dominate and terrify all other birds (the people of Rome). He thinks that, by influencing the people, the tribunes can limit Caesar's power.

75. *ordinary pitch:* at a moderate height. The 'pitch' was strictly the height from which a falcon swooped down on its prey. This image from falconry carries on from line 74.

77. *in servile fearfulness:* like frightened slaves.

To hear the replication of your sounds
Made in her concave shores?
And do you now put on your best attire?   *50*
And do you now cull out a holiday?
And do you now strew flowers in his way
That comes in triumph over Pompey's blood?
Be gone!
Run to your houses, fall upon your knees,   *55*
Pray to the gods to intermit the plague
That needs must light on this ingratitude.

Flavius

Go, go, good countrymen, and for this fault
Assemble all the poor men of your sort;
Draw them to Tiber banks, and weep your tears   *60*
Into the channel, till the lowest stream
Do kiss the most exalted shores of all.

Exeunt all the COMMONERS

See whe'r their basest metal be not mov'd;
They vanish tongue-tied in their guiltiness.

Go you down that way towards the Capitol;   *65*
This way will I. Disrobe the images
If you do find them deck'd with ceremonies.

Marullus

May we do so?
You know it is the feast of Lupercal.

Flavius

It is no matter; let no images   *70*
Be hung with Caesar's trophies. I'll about,
And drive away the vulgar from the streets;
So do you too, where you perceive them thick.
These growing feathers pluck'd from Caesar's wing
Will make him fly an ordinary pitch,   *75*
Who else would soar above the view of men,
And keep us all in servile fearfulness.

Exeunt

SCENE II

The great Caesar appears, but within two or three minutes, perhaps rather disappointingly, he has gone again. In these fleeting moments, Shakespeare gives us impressions of him that are slightly contradictory, rather vague and by no means agreeable. Caesar seems to believe in one form of superstition but dismisses another almost with contempt. He gives no fewer than six clear commands in the first few words he utters and the response he receives, at least from one character, is worship and flattery. He seems to be an aloof, distant and impersonal figure and the impression is all the stronger because of the short period of time that he is seen. We do not know quite what to make of him but we cannot really like what we see.

But the bulk of the scene is made up of a conversation between Brutus and Cassius. This, the beginning of a conspiracy against Caesar, is interesting not so much for what it tells us about Caesar, who is the subject of the conversation, as for what we learn about Cassius, the man who does most of the talking and who actually launches the conspiracy. It is necessary to try to sift the truth about Caesar, about Brutus, about Rome and about Cassius himself from the passionately expressed but very biased ideas that Cassius pours out. The same applies when, after Caesar has come and gone again (and in the process given his own very shrewd judgment on Cassius), Casca reports what all the shouting was about. Here, we must try to distinguish the truth from what has been twisted by Casca's eccentricity or by his own dislike of Caesar.

5. *run his course:* his run through the streets as part of the Lupercal celebrations. He would carry a leather whip and, according to the superstition of the Roman era, barren women would be made fertile if struck by the whip of one of the athletes.

8. *our elders say.* Perhaps Caesar is reluctant to let it be thought that he believes this personally.

11. See what instant obedience Caesar commands. (Or, at least, Antony willingly shows.)

SCENE II—*Rome. A public place*

> *Music. Enter* CAESAR; ANTONY, *for the course;*
> CALPHURNIA, PORTIA, DECIUS, CICERO, BRUTUS,
> CASSIUS, *and* CASCA; *a great crowd following, among*
> *them a* SOOTHSAYER; *after them,* MARULLUS *and*
> FLAVIUS

Caesar
  Calphurnia.
Casca   Peace, ho! Caesar speaks.

Music ceases

Caesar
  Calphurnia.
Calphurnia
  Here, my lord.
Caesar
  Stand you directly in Antonius' way
  When he doth run his course. Antonius!   5
Antony
  Caesar, my lord.
Caesar
  Forget not in your speed, Antonius,
  To touch Calphurnia; for our elders say,
  The barren, touched in this holy chase,
  Shake off their sterile curse.
Antony   I shall remember.   10
  When Caesar says 'Do this', it is perform'd.
Caesar
  Set on, and leave no ceremony out.

Music

Soothsayer
  Caesar!

31

16. *press:* the crowd pressing round Caesar.

18. Caesar doesn't say '*I* am turned to hear' but speaks of himself in the third person. Caesar's use of the expression makes him appear very arrogant. Similar signs of his haughtiness can be found from time to time. On the other hand, it can be argued that, considering his position and his achievements, he is only speaking in a way that is natural and to be expected of him.

20. *Ides of March:* March 15, according to our calendar. Properly presented, the event described here should be vivid and highly dramatic with the soothsayer's voice rising shrilly above the hubbub of the crowd. The fact that the warning is uttered no fewer than three times makes it seem particularly ominous.

25. *Pass:* pass on, continue the procession.

26. *order of the course:* how the race goes.

29. *gamesome:* fond of games.

30. *quick spirit:* 'active disposition' and also 'speed in the race'.

31-2. Clearly, Brutus is uneasy about something.

Caesar
  Ha! Who calls?
Casca
  Bid every noise be still. Peace yet again.   *15*

                    Music ceases

Caesar
  Who is it in the press that calls on me?
  I hear a tongue, shriller than all the music,
  Cry 'Caesar!' Speak. Caesar is turn'd to hear.
Soothsayer
  Beware the ides of March.
Caesar   What man is that?
Brutus
  A soothsayer bids you beware the ides of March.   *20*
Caesar
  Set him before me; let me see his face.
Cassius
  Fellow, come from the throng; look upon Caesar.
Caesar
  What say'st thou to me now? Speak once again.
Soothsayer
  Beware the ides of March.
Caesar
  He is a dreamer; let us leave him. Pass.   *25*

        Sennet. Exeunt all but BRUTUS *and* CASSIUS

Cassius
  Will you go see the order of the course?
Brutus
  Not I.
Cassius
  I pray you do.
Brutus
  I am not gamesome: I do lack some part
  Of that quick spirit that is in Antony.   *30*
  Let me not hinder, Cassius, your desires;

36-7. *You bear . . . loves you:* 'You have been treating your firm friend (myself) too harshly and been too cold towards him.' Cassius expresses himself in terms of a rider who treats his horse roughly.

38-43. *If I have veiled . . . behaviours:* 'If I have avoided you, it has been in order to make myself, rather than you, bear the brunt of my bad temper. I have been troubled recently with conflicting feelings, thoughts that concern me alone, and they have had a bad effect on my conduct.'

46-8. *Nor construe . . . other men.* Brutus asks Cassius simply to interpret his behaviour by understanding that his personal problems make him fail to show respect for other people. He obviously wishes to be left alone with his difficulties.

49. *passion:* usually, this means 'anger' but in this case, 'anxiety' or just strong feelings generally.

50-1. *By means . . . value:* 'For this reason, I have kept to myself some important ideas.'

51. *cogitations:* thoughts; considerations.

52. Here, and in the following speech, Cassius says that just as a person needs a mirror to see his own face, so Brutus needs somebody else to explain and interpret his own emotions.

54. *But by . . . things:* 'Except by means of something else that can reflect his image.'

55. *just:* true.

58. *Your hidden . . . eye:* 'Reveal your good qualities for your own inspection.'

59. *shadow:* reflection.

60. *best respect:* highest quality. Cassius hints that there is an important anti-Caesar group in Rome.

61. *immortal Caesar.* Cassius must be using the word 'immortal' sarcastically here.

62. *yoke:* the piece of wood which holds a draught animal under control: a symbol of the oppression existing in Rome.

63. *had his eyes:* 'could understand the situation as clearly as himself.'

34

I'll leave you.
Cassius
  Brutus, I do observe you now of late;
  I have not from your eyes that gentleness
  And show of love as I was wont to have.   *35*
  You bear too stubborn and too strange a hand
  Over your friend that loves you.
Brutus   Cassius,
  Be not deceiv'd. If I have veil'd my look,
  I turn the trouble of my countenance
  Merely upon myself. Vexed I am   *40*
  Of late with passions of some difference,
  Conceptions only proper to myself,
  Which give some soil, perhaps, to my behaviours;
  But let not therefore my good friends be griev'd—
  Among which number, Cassius, be you one—   *45*
  Nor construe any further my neglect
  Than that poor Brutus, with himself at war,
  Forgets the shows of love to other men.
Cassius
  Then, Brutus, I have much mistook your passion,
  By means whereof this breast of mine hath buried   *50*
  Thoughts of great value, worthy cogitations.
  Tell me, good Brutus, can you see your face?
Brutus
  No, Cassius; for the eye sees not itself
  But by reflection, by some other things.
Cassius
  'Tis just;   *55*
  And it is very much lamented, Brutus,
  That you have no such mirrors as will turn
  Your hidden worthiness into your eye,
  That you might see your shadow. I have heard,
  Where many of the best respect in Rome—   *60*
  Except immortal Caesar—speaking of Brutus,
  And groaning underneath this age's yoke,
  Have wish'd that noble Brutus had his eyes.

64-6. Brutus seems to be pretending ignorance of Cassius's intentions. This comment is apparently an invitation to Cassius to put his cards on the table. Cassius's 'therefore' means, in effect, 'All right, then, I'll tell you everything'.

69. *glass:* mirror.

70. *modestly discover:* reveal in a fair or reasonable way.

72. *jealous on:* suspicious of.

73-5. *Were 1 . . . protester:* 'If I were a general laughing-stock or were in the habit of cheapening myself by swearing friendship towards everybody who claims to like me . . .'

76. *fawn on . . . hard:* 'make a fuss of (flatter) people and become bosom friends.'

77. *scandal:* slander.

78-9. *profess . . . all the rout:* 'declare my friendship for all the riff-raff (common people) while under the influence of drink.'

Stage Direction. *Flourish and shout.* The 'flourish' is a blast of sound from trumpets. These distant sounds of the crowd and of the celebrations constantly remind us of the cause of this furtive conversation.

81. Cassius seizes on Brutus's quite mild expression of concern in order to get to the real point of the talk.

86-90. *If it be . . . fear death:* 'If it is something concerning the good of all the people of Rome, then I will regard honour and death quite impartially. May I thrive only in so far as I put the principle of honour before my fear of death.' This passage provides the clue to nearly all Brutus's important actions and decisions in the play.

92. *favour:* appearance.

Brutus

    Into what dangers would you lead me, Cassius,

    That you would have me seek into myself   65

    For that which is not in me?

Cassius

    Therefore, good Brutus, be prepar'd to hear;

    And since you know you cannot see yourself

    So well as by reflection, I, your glass,

    Will modestly discover to yourself   70

    That of yourself which you yet know not of.

    And be not jealous on me, gentle Brutus:

    Were I a common laughter, or did use

    To stale with ordinary oaths my love

    To every new protester; if you know   75

    That I do fawn on men and hug them hard,

    And after scandal them; or if you know

    That I profess myself in banqueting

    To all the rout, then hold me dangerous.

Flourish and shout

Brutus

    What means this shouting? I do fear the people   80

    Choose Caesar for their king.

Cassius   Ay, do you fear it?

    Then must I think you would not have it so.

Brutus

    I would not, Cassius; yet I love him well.

    But wherefore do you hold me here so long?

    What is it that you would impart to me?   85

    If it be aught toward the general good,

    Set honour in one eye and death i' th' other,

    And I will look on both indifferently;

    For let the gods so speed me as I love

    The name of honour more than I fear death.   90

Cassius

    I know that virtue to be in you, Brutus,

    As well as I do know your outward favour.

96-7. *I had as lief . . . I myself:* 'I would rather die than live in fear of a mere human being.' The attitude revealed in this speech is rather different from that shown by Brutus, who is chiefly concerned about the 'general good' and questions of 'honour'. Cassius just seems determined to belittle a man he is jealous of. He seems to think that Caesar's reputation can be stained by the fact that he once came off second-best in a swimming match or because he was once ill on campaign. But we must remember that Caesar, in the opinion of his opponents, had achieved almost god-like status in Rome, and Cassius's words are intended to show him as a mere mortal after all.

102. *chafing:* 'rushing' or 'scouring' angrily.

103. *Dar'st thou:* 'would you dare?'

106. *Accoutred:* fully clothed.

110. *stemming . . . controversy:* 'thrusting against the flood, eager to beat it and one another as well.'

113-15. Cassius tries to emphasize Caesar's weakness by comparing him with the old and feeble Anchises (father of Aeneas in the Latin poet Virgil's epic poem *The Aeneid*), who had to be carried out of the burning city of Troy by his son.

117-19. Note that Cassius shows *personal* resentment against Caesar, in contrast to Brutus's less selfish attitude.

123. Cassius's hatred and indignation make him describe how Caesar's face and lips lost their natural red colour and grew pale. But the metaphor also suggests the idea of a soldier deserting his standard ('colour') in battle and running away. The combination of these ideas is rather forced but no doubt makes its point.

124. *bend:* look, glance.

125. *lustre:* sparkle, natural healthy appearance.

126-7. Caesar was an able orator but note that Cassius implies arrogance on Caesar's part by saying that he had *told* the people to take down notes of his speeches, rather like a teacher with his pupils.

Well, honour is the subject of my story.
I cannot tell what you and other men
Think of this life; but, for my single self,   *95*
I had as lief not be as live to be
In awe of such a thing as I myself.
I was born free as Caesar; so were you.
We both have fed as well, and we can both
Endure the winter's cold as well as he.   *100*
For once, upon a raw and gusty day,
The troubled Tiber chafing with her shores,
Caesar said to me 'Dar'st thou, Cassius, now
Leap in with me into this angry flood,
And swim to yonder point?' Upon the word,   *105*
Accoutred as I was, I plunged in
And bade him follow. So indeed he did.
The torrent roar'd, and we did buffet it
With lusty sinews, throwing it aside
And stemming it with hearts of controversy;   *110*
But ere we could arrive the point propos'd,
Caesar cried, 'Help me, Cassius, or I sink!'
I, as Aeneas, our great ancestor,
Did from the flames of Troy upon his shoulder
The old Anchises bear, so from the waves of Tiber   *115*
Did I the tired Caesar. And this man
Is now become a god; and Cassius is
A wretched creature, and must bend his body
If Caesar carelessly but nod on him.
He had a fever when he was in Spain,   *120*
And when the fit was on him I did mark
How he did shake. 'Tis true, this god did shake.
His coward lips did from their colour fly,
And that same eye, whose bend doth awe the world,
Did lose his lustre. I did hear him groan.   *125*
Ay, and that tongue of his, that bade the Romans
Mark him, and write his speeches in their books,
Alas! it cried 'Give me some drink, Titinius'
As a sick girl. Ye gods! it doth amaze me

130. *feeble temper:* poor quality.

131-2. *get the start . . . alone:* 'take the lead in the race and carry off the prize.' The palm was the Roman symbol of victory in a race and the winner would actually be crowned with palm leaves.

133-6. Brutus had obviously been disturbed enough by the previous shout (line 79) to comment on it. Cassius seems to feel that this second shout is an opportunity to press his argument even harder.

137. *Colossus:* a gigantic statue, said to have straddled the entrance to the harbour at Rhodes, though this is unlikely. It came to be used as a symbol for anything of great size and to Cassius it is a good object of comparison as it conveys a sense of vast power.

141. *our stars.* Elizabethans believed that the position and movements of stars at the time of a man's birth determined his life and destiny. This was the basis of the popular science of astrology which had existed since very ancient times. Cassius's view expresses the more modern idea of freewill which says that a man can carve out his own destiny.

144. *sounded:* spoken; but the word here suggests 'proclaimed' in public, as Caesar's often was.

147. *Conjure with 'em.* This refers to the practice of summoning up spirits from the underworld by the use of words or chants, including the name of a god—a kind of 'black magic'.

148. 'The name of Caesar has no more power than yours to raise spirits.'

150-1. Cassius's contempt suggests that Caesar must have been eating some special food for him to become so 'big'.

151. *Age, thou art sham'd!* 'What a disgrace to our generation.'

152. *Rome . . . bloods.* He means that Rome has lost the capacity to rear men of character and spirit.

153. *great flood:* not the flood referred to in the Bible but another one mentioned in Classical mythology.

154. *But it was fam'd . . . one man:* 'Which wasn't famous because of many men rather than just one.'

157. *Rome* and *room* would probably have been pronounced alike, thus making a pun.

160-2. This refers to an ancestor of Brutus who drove out a tyrant, Tarquin—a noble act that Brutus would have been proud of, and thus a powerful argument in the attempt to stir up Brutus against Caesar.

A man of such a feeble temper should   *130*
So get the start of the majestic world,
And bear the palm alone.

Shout.   Flourish

Brutus
Another general shout!
I do believe that these applauses are
For some new honours that are heap'd on Caesar.   *135*
Cassius
Why, man, he doth bestride the narrow world
Like a Colossus, and we petty men
Walk under his huge legs, and peep about
To find ourselves dishonourable graves.
Men at some time are masters of their fates: *140*
The fault, dear Brutus, is not in our stars,
But in ourselves, that we are underlings.
'Brutus' and 'Caesar'. What should be in that
    'Caesar'?
Why should that name be sounded more than yours?
Write them together; yours is as fair a name.   *145*
Sound them: it doth become the mouth as well.
Weigh them: it is as heavy. Conjure with 'em:
'Brutus' will start a spirit as soon as 'Caesar'.
Now, in the names of all the gods at once,
Upon what meat doth this our Caesar feed,   *150*
That he is grown so great? Age, thou art sham'd!
Rome, thou has lost the breed of noble bloods!
When went there by an age, since the great flood,
But it was fam'd with more than with one man?
When could they say, till now, that talk'd of Rome,   *155*
That her wide walls encompass'd but one man?
Now is it Rome indeed, and room enough,
When there is in it but one only man.
O! you and I have heard our fathers say
There was a Brutus once that would have brook'd   *160*

161. *eternal.* The word has a vague but strongly derogatory sense. Cassius means that Brutus's ancestor would have tolerated the devil himself in Rome in preference to such a tyrant as a king. Owing to their unhappy experiences under kings in their history, the Romans dreaded the very name, which stood for what we would call dictatorship.

163-4. *That you . . . aim:* 'I have no doubt that you speak in true friendship and I can guess what you want me to do.'

167. *so with . . . entreat you:* 'if I may ask this favour.'

168. *mov'd:* urged, pressed.

171. *meet:* suitable, fitting.

172. *chew upon:* ponder, consider.

173. *villager:* a peasant; someone of low social status, not a true Roman citizen.

176. *like:* likely.

177-8. The figure of speech here is taken from the old method of making a spark to light a fire, i.e. by means of tinder and flint. Is Cassius disappointed or satisfied by Brutus's apparently cool reaction?

Stage Direction. *train:* retinue; party of guards and followers.

181. *sour fashion:* surly manner.

182. 'What's happened of importance today.'

184. *angry spot:* an inflamed patch.

185. *chidden:* scolded, rebuked.

187. *ferret:* ferrety, i.e. with eyes like a ferret's, because they are bloodshot with anger. A ferret is a long, low mammal, domesticated and trained to hunt rabbits and rats.

189. *conference:* debate, argument.

Th' eternal devil to keep his state in Rome
As easily as a king.

Brutus

That you do love me, I am nothing jealous;
What you would work me to, I have some aim;
How I have thought of this, and of these times,   *165*
I shall recount hereafter. For this present,
I would not, so with love I might entreat you,
Be any further mov'd. What you have said
I will consider; what you have to say
I will with patience hear; and find a time   *170*
Both meet to hear and answer such high things.
Till then, my noble friend, chew upon this:
Brutus had rather be a villager
Than to repute himself a son of Rome
Under these hard conditions as this time   *175*
Is like to lay upon us.

Cassius

I am glad that my weak words
Have struck but thus much show of fire from Brutus.

Re-enter CAESAR *and his* TRAIN

Brutus

The games are done, and Caesar is returning.

Cassius

As they pass by, pluck Casca by the sleeve,   *180*
And he will, after his sour fashion, tell you
What hath proceeded worthy note to-day.

Brutus

I will do so. But, look you, Cassius,
The angry spot doth glow on Caesar's brow,
And all the rest look like a chidden train;   *185*
Calphurnia's cheek is pale, and Cicero
Looks with such ferret and such fiery eyes
As we have seen him in the Capitol,
Being cross'd in conference by some senators.

43

194. *Sleek-headed:* with smooth, unruffled hair, indicating contentment.

196-7. Caesar correctly picks out his bitterest enemy. Antony doesn't agree, but ironically Cassius is the one who wants to murder both Antony and Caesar later in the play (Act II, Scene i, lines 155-7).

198. *well given:* amiable.

199. Caesar clearly regards fat people as easy-going and contented, while leanness, to him, is a sign of jealousy and bitterness.

200. *Yet if . . . fear:* 'If it were possible for Caesar to feel fear.' He seems rather anxious to assert that he is not afraid. Is this because he really is afraid? Watch for later occasions when his courage might be questioned.

202. *spare:* thin.

203-4. *looks Quite . . . men:* can spot men's true motives; he can 'see through' them.

206. *sort:* manner.

210. Caesar is probably right in diagnosing Cassius's *lean and hungry look* as the result of jealousy. We have just seen evidence of this in the conversation with Brutus.

212-13. Again Caesar emphasizes, not wholly necessarily, his immunity to fear.

214. This is the first indication that Caesar suffers from any infirmity (apart, possibly, from *Caesar is turned to hear* at the beginning of this scene). Of course, deafness in one ear is not a serious defect in itself but this, plus the more serious epilepsy which we learn about later, does not exactly accord with the atmosphere of infallibility and power that surrounds Caesar. Later, when both Calphurnia and Decius Brutus give Caesar contradictory advice on whether he should go to the Senate, he is, in another sense, deaf in one ear.

216. We have had a long spell of tense and absorbing drama, written in blank verse. Shakespeare now relaxes into prose, more suitable for Casca's colloquial style of speaking, and for the drop in tension after Caesar's exit.

Cassius
  Casca will tell us what the matter is.   *190*

Caesar
  Antonius!

Antony
  Caesar?

Caesar
  Let me have men about me that are fat;
  Sleek-headed men, and such as sleep o' nights.
  Yond Cassius has a lean and hungry look;   *195*
  He thinks too much. Such men are dangerous.

Antony
  Fear him not, Caesar, he's not dangerous;
  He is a noble Roman, and well given.

Caesar
  Would he were fatter! But I fear him not.
  Yet if my name were liable to fear,   *200*
  I do not know the man I should avoid
  So soon as that spare Cassius. He reads much,
  He is a great observer, and he looks
  Quite through the deeds of men. He loves no plays,
  As thou dost, Antony; he hears no music.   *205*
  Seldom he smiles, and smiles in such a sort
  As if he mock'd himself, and scorn'd his spirit
  That could be mov'd to smile at anything.
  Such men as he be never at heart's ease
  Whiles they behold a greater than themselves,   *210*
  And therefore are they very dangerous.
  I rather tell thee what is to be fear'd
  Than what I fear; for always I am Caesar.
  Come on my right hand, for this ear is deaf,
  And tell me truly what thou think'st of him.   *215*

          Sennet. Exeunt CAESAR *and his* TRAIN

Casca
  You pull'd me by the cloak. Would you speak with
  me?

45

219. *sad:* grave, serious.

223. *put it by:* pushed it aside.

230-1. *every . . . other:* each time more gently than before.

232. *honest.* Normally in Shakespeare, this means 'morally good' or 'decent'. Here, Casca must intend some sarcasm, in view of his other comments about the crowd.

236-7. *I can . . . mark it:* 'I'm hanged if I can describe it. It was nonsense, really. I didn't take much notice.'

240-1. *to my thinking . . . had it:* 'I think he really wanted to have it'.

Brutus

  Ay, Casca; tell us what hath chanc'd to-day,
  That Caesar looks so sad?

Casca

  Why, you were with him, were you not?   *220*

Brutus

  I should not then ask Casca what had chanc'd.

Casca

  Why, there was a crown offer'd him; and being offer'd
  him, he put it by with the back of his hand, thus; and
  then the people fell a-shouting.

Brutus

  What was the second noise for?   *225*

Casca

  Why, for that too.

Cassius

  They shouted thrice; what was the last cry for?

Casca

  Why, for that too.

Brutus

  Was the crown offer'd him thrice?

Casca

  Ay, marry, was't, and he put it by thrice, every time *230*
  gentler than other; and at every putting by mine
  honest neighbours shouted.

Cassius

  Who offer'd him the crown?

Casca

  Why, Antony.

Brutus

  Tell us the manner of it, gentle Casca.   *235*

Casca

  I can as well be hang'd as tell the manner of it: it was
  mere foolery; I did not mark it. I saw Mark Antony
  offer him a crown—yet 'twas not a crown neither, 'twas
  one of these coronets—and, as I told you, he put it by
  once; but for all that, to my thinking, he would fain *240*

Casca repeats this idea a sentence or two later. He may be right in thinking that Caesar was reluctant to refuse the crown, or he may simply be expressing his own dislike for Caesar.

245. *rabblement:* rabble, unruly mob.
chopt: chapped, rough (from work).

249. *swooned:* fainted.

250. Casca's 'laugh', of course, would be a laugh of ridicule or contempt at the crowd's folly and stupidity.

255. *'Tis very like:* 'that's quite likely'.
falling sickness: epilepsy. Clearly, Brutus already knows about Caesar's illness. Cassius deliberately takes the expression literally to indicate how he and his friends have 'fallen' under the power of Caesar.

259. *tag-rag:* an expression of vague meaning, probably suggesting 'ragged'.

261-2. *as they use . . . theatre:* 'as they are accustomed to do to the actors.'

266. *pluckt me ope:* 'pulled his doublet open' (the word *me* is a superfluous survival from an old grammatical form).

267-9. *An I had been . . . rogues:* 'If I had been a man of action (or, if I had been a working man), I would have done as he asked or gladly gone to hell if I hadn't.' Casca is just saying that he would have liked to cut Caesar's throat.

have had it. Then he offered it to him again; then he
put it by again; but to my thinking, he was very loath
to lay his fingers off it. And then he offered it the third
time; he put it the third time by; and still as he refus'd
it, the rabblement hooted, and clapp'd their chopt 245
hands, and threw up their sweaty night-caps, and
uttered such a deal of stinking breath because Caesar
refus'd the crown, that it had almost choked Caesar;
for he swooned and fell down at it. And for mine
own part I durst not laugh, for fear of opening my 250
lips and receiving the bad air.

Cassius

But soft, I pray you. What, did Caesar swoon?

Casca

He fell down in the market-place, and foam'd at
mouth, and was speechless.

Brutus

'Tis very like. He hath the falling sickness. 255

Cassius

No, Caesar hath it not; but you, and I,
And honest Casca, we have the falling sickness.

Casca

I know not what you mean by that, but I am sure
Caesar fell down. If the tag-rag people did not clap
him and hiss him, according as he pleas'd and dis- 260
pleas'd them, as they use to do the players in the
theatre, I am no true man.

Brutus

What said he when he came unto himself?

Casca

Marry, before he fell down, when he perceiv'd the
common herd was glad he refus'd the crown, he 265
pluckt me ope his doublet, and offer'd them his throat
to cut. An I had been a man of any occupation, if I
would not have taken him at a word, I would I might
go to hell among the rogues. And so he fell. When he
came to himself again, he said, if he had done or said 270

271. *their worships:* a sarcastic comment. Casca deliberately exaggerates and sneers at Caesar's humble manner towards the crowd.

277. *sad:* grave, serious.

280. Cicero would be familiar with Greek, which was a language learned by most well-educated men in Rome. He seems to have said something that he wanted only his learned friends to understand.

282-3. *Nay, an . . . face again:* probably because the comment was an uncomplimentary remark about Caesar and therefore dangerous to repeat. Though Casca says shortly afterwards that he didn't understand what Cicero said, he could probably guess at its meaning.

285. *It was Greek to me:* a phrase with much the same meaning as it has today—I didn't understand it.

287. *put to silence.* This sinister phrase probably means that they were executed for opposing Caesar. The *scarfs* would be some kind of decoration to celebrate Caesar's triumphant return to Rome (see Act I, Scene i, line 65).

289-91. These invitations are presumably to give Cassius an opportunity of sounding Casca more carefully about his attitude to Caesar and of drawing him into the conspiracy.

292-3. 'Yes, if I'm alive then and you still want me to come and can provide a good meal.' This is a good example of Casca's eccentric and cynical manner.

anything amiss, he desir'd their worships to think it
was his infirmity. Three or four wenches, where I
stood, cried 'Alas, good soul!' and forgave him with
all their hearts. But there's no heed to be taken of
them; if Caesar had stabb'd their mothers, they 275
would have done no less.

Brutus

And after that, he came thus sad away?

Casca

Ay.

Cassius

Did Cicero say anything?

Casca

Ay, he spoke Greek. 280

Cassius

To what effect?

Casca

Nay, an I tell you that, I'll ne'er look you i' th' face
again. But those that understood him smil'd at one
another, and shook their heads; but for mine own
part, it was Greek to me. I could tell you more news 285
too: Marullus and Flavius, for pulling scarfs off
Caesar's images, are put to silence. Fare you well.
There was more foolery yet, if I could remember it.

Cassius

Will you sup with me to-night, Casca?

Casca

No, I am promis'd forth. 290

Cassius

Will you dine with me to-morrow?

Casca

Ay, if I be alive, and your mind hold, and your
dinner worth the eating.

Cassius

Good; I will expect you.

Casca

Do so. Farewell, both. 295

297. *quick mettle:* a lively character, a 'bright spark'.

300. *tardy form:* dull manner; appearance of being slow on the uptake.
rudeness: a gruff manner rather than offensiveness.
301. *wit:* intelligence.
Cassius says that this blunt manner of speaking is like a sharp sauce to a good meal. It enables men to relish and appreciate his words better.

308. *think of the world:* 'consider the state of the world.' Cassius is anxious not to let Brutus forget the disturbing issues they have discussed.

309-11. *yet, I see . . . dispos'd:* 'I see it is possible to make you do something you are not really inclined to.' The metaphor is from metalwork, Cassius saying that he can shape or mould Brutus's character just as metal can be bent or hammered into a different form.

314. *doth bear me hard:* has a grudge against me.
314-16. A difficult and important passage, the meaning of which largely depends on whether the word *he* (line 315) refers to Caesar or Cassius. The simplest interpretation is to assume that it means Cassius; in other words, Cassius is saying that if he and Brutus were to exchange places, Cassius wouldn't allow himself to be influenced or played with as Brutus is being by Cassius. It is true that this shows a contemptuous attitude towards Brutus that is not apparent elsewhere in the play. But Cassius is certainly presented as a bitter and unscrupulous man, capable of cynical contempt in most directions.
316. *humour me:* influence me by playing on my moods and wishes.
317. *several hands:* the handwriting of various people.
319. *tending to:* concerning.
320-1. *wherein . . . glanced at:* 'in these, subtle criticisms will be made of Caesar's love of power.'
322. *let Caesar seat him sure:* 'Caesar had better look after himself carefully.'

Exit

Brutus
What a blunt fellow is this grown to be!
He was quick mettle when he went to school.
Cassius
So is he now, in execution
Of any bold or noble enterprise,
However he puts on this tardy form.   *300*
This rudeness is a sauce to his good wit,
Which gives men stomach to digest his words
With better appetite.
Brutus
And so it is. For this time I will leave you.
To-morrow, if you please to speak with me,   *305*
I will come home to you; or, if you will,
Come home to me, and I will wait for you.
Cassius
I will do so. Till then, think of the world.

Exit BRUTUS

Well, Brutus, thou art noble; yet, I see,
Thy honourable metal may be wrought   *310*
From that it is dispos'd. Therefore it is meet
That noble minds keep ever with their likes;
For who so firm that cannot be seduc'd?
Caesar doth bear me hard; but he loves Brutus.
If I were Brutus now and he were Cassius,   *315*
He should not humour me. I will this night,
In several hands, in at his windows throw,
As if they came from several citizens,
Writings, all tending to the great opinion
That Rome holds of his name; wherein obscurely   *320*
Caesar's ambition shall be glanced at.
And, after this, let Caesar seat him sure;
For we will shake him, or worse days endure.

Exit

SCENE III

In this scene, discontent and conflict in the world of men is given its counterpart in the world of Nature—a violent thunderstorm. This is no ordinary storm and its violence and the extraordinary events that accompany it would be recognized by the Elizabethan audience as a bad omen, even if this fact were not pointed out clearly in the text of the play. However, Cassius himself (though his own philosophy would tell him that the storm has no significance) uses it to convince Casca that the gods have a special purpose in making it happen in this way and at this particular time. He has not been slow in other ways and with other people in his attempts to raise support for a conspiracy against Caesar but the last ten lines of the scene warn us that the whole plan will not be on a sure footing unless and until one very important person can be persuaded to join and lead them.

3-4. *sway of earth . . . infirm:* 'the well-founded earth trembles like a leaf.' We now see a frightened and very different Casca from the rough-and-ready character of the previous scene.

6. *riv'd:* split open.

8. *exalted with:* raised to.

12. *saucy:* insolent. Casca's belief is that the terrible storm in which, as it seems, it is 'raining fire', must indicate either a quarrel amongst the gods themselves, or their anger because of man's contempt for them.

14. Cicero's reply is coldly polite: 'Nothing more sensational than that?' Cicero, the intellectual, doesn't share Casca's superstitious fears.

15-17. This is probably an example of St. Elmo's fire which is rare but not unknown in violent thunderstorms. In this phenomenon the rigging of ships, for example, is sometimes outlined by an electrical discharge.

18. *Not sensible of fire:* not feeling the heat.

19. *put up:* put away, sheathed.

20. *Against:* by, near to.

22. *annoying:* harming.

22-3. *and there . . . ghastly women:* 'there were a hundred white-faced women, huddled together.'

26. *bird of night:* the Barn Owl or screech-owl. The owl has often been regarded as a bird of bad omen.

SCENE III—*Rome. A street*

Thunder and lightning.   Enter, from opposite sides,
CASCA, *with his sword drawn, and* CICERO

Cicero
    Good even, Casca. Brought you Caesar home?
    Why are you breathless? and why stare you so?
Casca
    Are not you mov'd, when all the sway of earth
    Shakes like a thing unfirm? O Cicero,
    I have seen tempests when the scolding winds   5
    Have riv'd the knotty oaks, and I have seen
    Th' ambitious ocean swell, and rage, and foam,
    To be exalted with the threat'ning clouds;
    But never till to-night, never till now,
    Did I go through a tempest dropping fire.   10
    Either there is a civil strife in heaven,
    Or else the world, too saucy with the gods,
    Incenses them to send destruction.
Cicero
    Why, saw you any thing more wonderful?
Casca
    A common slave—you know him well by sight—   15
    Held up his left hand, which did flame and burn
    Like twenty torches join'd; and yet his hand,
    Not sensible of fire, remain'd unscorch'd.
    Besides—I ha' not since put up my sword—
    Against the Capitol I met a lion,   20
    Who glar'd upon me, and went surly by
    Without annoying me; and there were drawn
    Upon a heap a hundred ghastly women,
    Transformed with their fear, who swore they saw
    Men, all in fire, walk up and down the streets.   25
    And yesterday the bird of night did sit,

28. *prodigies:* ominous events, portents.

29. *conjointly meet:* come together, coincide.

29-30. *let not . . . natural:* 'men cannot possibly say that such and such are the explanations, that they are perfectly natural events.'

31-2. 'For I believe they are bad omens for the country in which they reveal themselves.' Casca's fear is caused by a number of extraordinary events that are, to him, signs of terrible disasters which will afflict the world of men in the near future, as well as being frightening in themselves. Though Cicero rejects Casca's interpretation, Casca would probably be expressing the popular view of Shakespeare's day, and Shakespeare frequently used such omens in his plays to indicate and prepare his audience for dire events to come in the drama, particularly the death or fall of a king or great man. Here, the implied reference to Caesar is obvious.

33. *strange-disposed time:* unusual weather, and also 'uncanny time.'

34-5. 'Men may interpret events in their own way, which is often a long way from the truth.'

39-40. Cicero's farewell is a frigidly polite rebuke to the terrified Casca. 'Well, good-bye, Casca. We mustn't stay out of doors on a night like this.'

43. *honest men:* men of honour. Cassius, we see, is delighted by the violent thunderstorm as he knows that many people would regard it as a dangerous omen for Caesar and he hopes to exploit this fact.

45. Cassius's reply to Casca's question says that the 'heavens' are indicating their displeasure at the corrupt state of Rome.

48. *unbraced:* with his doublet (a kind of Elizabethan jacket) unbuttoned.

49. *thunderstone:* thunderbolt.

50. *cross blue lightning:* forked lightning.

Even at noon-day, upon the market-place,
Hooting and shrieking. When these prodigies
Do so conjointly meet, let not men say
'These are their reasons—they are natural',   30
For I believe they are portentous things
Unto the climate that they point upon.

Cicero

Indeed, it is a strange-disposed time;
But men may construe things after their fashion,
Clean from the purpose of the things themselves.   35
Comes Caesar to the Capitol to-morrow?

Casca

He doth; for he did bid Antonius
Send word to you he would be there to-morrow.

Cicero

Good night, then, Casca; this disturbed sky
Is not to walk in.

Casca   Farewell, Cicero.   40

Exit CICERO. *Enter* CASSIUS

Cassius

Who's there?

Casca   A Roman.

Cassius   Casca, by your voice.

Casca

Your ear is good. Cassius, what night is this!

Cassius

A very pleasing night to honest men.

Casca

Who ever knew the heavens menace so?

Cassius

Those that have known the earth so full of faults.   45
For my part, I have walk'd about the streets,
Submitting me unto the perilous night,
And, thus unbraced, Casca, as you see,
Have bar'd my bosom to the thunderstone;
And when the cross blue lightning seem'd to open   50

57

52. *Even . . . flash of it.* He means that he tried to put himself in its path, inviting it to strike him. This display of bravado is Cassius's way of welcoming the arrival of divine judgment on Rome. It also shows the peculiar fascination that death holds for him though here he is really showing off rather than actually inviting the storm to kill him.

54. *part:* function, duty.

55. *tokens:* signs.

56. *astonish:* amaze, astound.

57-9. *those sparks . . . use not:* 'You either lack the imagination that a Roman should have, or you won't use the imagination you've got.'

60. *cast . . . wonder:* 'throw yourself into a state of doubt and amazement.'

62-71. This is a difficult speech which some editors have emended in order to make sense of it and some have even suggested that part of it is missing. However, we must remember that Cassius is speaking excitedly and therefore not quite logically or accurately. It is possible to make a reasonable paraphrase as follows: 'But if you would only consider the real reason for these flames, these ghosts flitting about, these birds and beasts acting quite contrary to their natural way of life; why doddering old men, half-wits and infants all seem able to make prophecies; why all these things, contrary to their proper functions, change their normal ways and original qualities to something fantastic —you will find that the gods have made them act this way to frighten us about something dreadful to come.' Note that Cassius, as shown later, does not believe in omens, at least until shortly before his death. Here, he is professing to believe in them for the sake of winning over Casca.

63-4. Cassius's hurried, agitated thought makes him miss out the main verbs in these two sentences.

65. *calculate:* prophesy.

66. *ordinance:* their proper way of life, as established by the gods or nature.

67. *preformed faculties:* qualities originally bestowed upon them.

71. *monstrous state:* abominable or horrifying situation.

75. *Capitol.* Lions were not kept in the Capitol at Rome but they *were* kept in the Tower of London in Shakespeare's day and Shakespeare's use of the word 'Capitol' suggests that he might be regarding this as the Roman equivalent of the Tower. But perhaps all Cassius is saying is, 'this man (Caesar) rants and raves in the Capitol like a roaring lion.'

77. *prodigious:* ominous, threatening.

78. *eruptions:* violent, unnatural events.

80. Cassius is clearly not yet sure enough of his ground to declare openly to Casca whom he has in mind.

81. *thews:* sinews.

The breast of heaven, I did present myself
Even in the aim and very flash of it.

Casca

But wherefore did you so much tempt the heavens?
It is the part of men to fear and tremble
When the most mighty gods by tokens send   55
Such dreadful heralds to astonish us.

Cassius

You are dull, Casca, and those sparks of life
That should be in a Roman you do want,
Or else you use not. You look pale, and gaze,
And put on fear, and cast yourself in wonder,   60
To see the strange impatience of the heavens;
But if you would consider the true cause—
Why all these fires, why all these gliding ghosts,
Why birds and beasts, from quality and kind;
Why old men, fools, and children calculate;   65
Why all these things change from their ordinance,
Their natures and preformed faculties,
To monstrous quality—why, you shall find
That heaven hath infus'd them with these spirits,
To make them instruments of fear and warning   70
Unto some monstrous state.
Now could I, Casca, name to thee a man
Most like this dreadful night
That thunders, lightens, opens graves, and roars
As doth the lion in the Capitol;   75
A man no mightier than thyself or me
In personal action, yet prodigious grown,
And fearful, as these strange eruptions are.

Casca

'Tis Caesar that you mean, is it not, Cassius?

Cassius

Let it be who it is; for Romans now   80
Have thews and limbs like to their ancestors.
But woe the while! our fathers' minds are dead,
And we are govern'd with our mothers' spirits;

84. 'Our mild and placid acceptance of this tyranny shows us to be effeminate.'

86. *king:* see Act I, Scene ii, line 162.

89. He means that he will commit suicide. This sentence, and the following lines in which he makes some elaborate and rather extravagant claims for the liberating power of death, again show Cassius's morbid preoccupation with the subject and his unstable temperament.
91. *Therein:* i.e. by means of the dagger.

95. 'Can contain a man of real spirit' (even though his body is shackled).
96. *worldly bars:* physical restraints.

98-100. *If I know . . . pleasure:* 'Since I know this, also let the whole world know that I can get rid of my particular share of the tyranny just when I wish (by killing myself)'.

101. *bondman:* servant or slave.
102. *cancel:* put an end to.

106. *hinds:* deer, and also 'slaves' or 'men of low class or quality'.
107-11. Cassius is condemning the people of Rome for being so feeble as to allow Caesar to dominate them. A man starting a big fire must begin with some light pieces of straw that will ignite easily; human material like this is at hand in Rome. (The words *trash*, *rubbish* and *offal* (the parts of an animal considered inedible by humans) all had the sense of something that is both worthless and easily burnt). This human 'rubbish' is the worthless stuff (*base matter*) that will serve to illuminate Caesar.

114. *My answer must be made:* 'I shall have to account for the dangerous things I have said.'

Our yoke and sufferance show us womanish.

Casca

    Indeed they say the senators to-morrow   *85*
    Mean to establish Caesar as a king;
    And he shall wear his crown by sea and land,
    In every place save here in Italy.

Cassius

    I know where I will wear this dagger then;
    Cassius from bondage will deliver Cassius.   *90*
    Therein, ye gods, you make the weak most strong
    Therein, ye gods, you tyrants do defeat.
    Nor stony tower, nor walls of beaten brass,
    Nor airless dungeon, nor strong links of iron,
    Can be retentive to the strength of spirit;   *95*
    But life, being weary of these worldly bars,
    Never lacks power to dismiss itself.
    If I know this, know all the world besides,
    That part of tyranny that I do bear,
    I can shake off at pleasure.

Thunder still

Casca   So can I;   *100*
    So every bondman in his own hand bears
    The power to cancel his captivity.

Cassius

    And why should Caesar be a tyrant, then?
    Poor man! I know he would not be a wolf
    But that he sees the Romans are but sheep;   *105*
    He were no lion, were not Romans hinds.
    Those that with haste will make a mighty fire
    Begin it with weak straws. What trash is Rome,
    What rubbish, and what offal, when it serves
    For the base matter to illuminate   *110*
    So vile a thing as Caesar! But, O grief,
    Where hast thou led me? I perhaps speak this
    Before a willing bondman; then I know
    My answer must be made. But I am arm'd,

61

115. *indifferent:* unimportant.

117. *fleering:* grinning; sneering.
hold, my hand. The punctuation shows that Casca is not actually asking Cassius to take his hand directly but just offering it in token of his good faith. 'Wait; let us shake hands on it.'
118-20. *Be factious . . . farthest:* 'If you start a conspiracy to settle these grievances, I'll go as far as anybody to put things right.'

121. *mov'd:* persuaded.

125. *by this:* by this time.
stay for: are waiting for.
126. *Pompey's porch:* the portal or entrance of the theatre built by Pompey the Great.
128-9. *the complexion . . . in hand:* 'the state of the sky, as it appears, is like the terrible work we have to do.'

131. *close:* aside (out of sight).

135-6. *one incorporate . . . attempts:* one who is already a member of the conspiracy.

137. *I am glad on't:* 'I am glad of it' (i.e. that Casca has joined).

And dangers are to me indifferent.   *115*
Casca
    You speak to Casca, and to such a man
    That is no fleering tell-tale. Hold, my hand.
    Be factious for redress of all these griefs,
    And I will set this foot of mine as far
    As who goes farthest.
Cassius   There's a bargain made.   *120*
    Now know you, Casca, I have mov'd already
    Some certain of the noblest-minded Romans
    To undergo with me an enterprise
    Of honourable-dangerous consequence;
    And I do know by this they stay for me   *125*
    In Pompey's porch; for now, this fearful night,
    There is no stir or walking in the streets,
    And the complexion of the element
    In favour's like the work we have in hand,
    Most bloody, fiery, and most terrible.   *130*

Enter CINNA

Casca
    Stand close awhile, for here comes one in haste.
Cassius
    'Tis Cinna, I do know him by his gait;
    He is a friend. Cinna, where haste you so?
Cinna
    To find out you. Who's that? Metellus Cimber?
Cassius
    No, it is Casca, one incorporate   *135*
    To our attempts. Am I not stay'd for, Cinna?
Cinna
    I am glad on't. What a fearful night is this!
    There's two or three of us have seen strange sights.
Cassius
    Am I not stay'd for? Tell me.
Cinna
    Yes, you are. O Cassius, if you could   *140*

144. *Where Brutus . . . find it:* Where only Brutus will find it. Cassius distributes various papers on which are written messages begging or encouraging Brutus to do something to free Rome from its oppression. Of course, these would be forgeries designed to convince Brutus that there was a much larger body of opposition to Caesar than really existed. This is an example of Cassius's ingenuity and unscrupulousness in persuading Brutus to join.

145. *set this up with wax:* stick it to the statue of Brutus with wax.

150. *hie:* hurry.

154-6. He means that Brutus has all but been 'captured' for the conspiracy, just like a besieged city that will fall completely at the next assault.

158. *offence:* an offensive or despicable act.

159. *countenance:* his presence amongst us, (literally, his 'face').

159-60. Alchemy was the early science which attempted (among other things) to change ordinary metals into gold. Though some alchemists were rogues, the whole practice of alchemy was for a long time highly regarded, and Cassius's figure of speech vividly expresses the great respect that people felt for Brutus and also the way in which, as they realised, his presence could transform the proposed murder from a brutal piece of treachery into a noble sacrifice for the good of all citizens.

162. *right well conceited:* very well understood and estimated.

But win the noble Brutus to our party—
Cassius

Be you content. Good Cinna, take this paper,
And look you lay it in the praetor's chair,
Where Brutus may but find it; and throw this
In at his window; set this up with wax   *145*
Upon old Brutus' statue. All this done,
Repair to Pompey's porch, where you shall find us.
Is Decius Brutus and Trebonius there?
Cinna

All but Metellus Cimber, and he's gone
To seek you at your house. Well, I will hie,   *150*
And so bestow these papers as you bade me.
Cassius

That done, repair to Pompey's theatre.

Exit CINNA

Come, Casca, you and I will yet ere day
See Brutus at his house. Three parts of him
Is ours already, and the man entire   *155*
Upon the next encounter yields him ours.
Casca

O, he sits high in all the people's hearts;
And that which would appear offence in us
His countenance, like richest alchemy,
Will change to virtue and to worthiness.   *160*
Cassius

Him and his worth and our great need of him
You have right well conceited. Let us go,
For it is after midnight; and ere day
We will awake him and be sure of him.

Exeunt

65

Brutus, then, is the uncertain factor on which the whole conspiracy now depends. Will he join? The answer is revealed in the scene that follows and it needs little imagination, especially in view of Cassius's confidence and cunning, to tell us what that decision will be. But what follows is interesting not so much for the decision as for the beliefs that inspire it, the reasoning that makes it possible and the conditions on which it is made. We have not seen very much of Brutus yet and if he is to be one of the major characters of the play (possibly even the 'hero'), Shakespeare has left it rather late before revealing him fully to us. We now hear Brutus in soliloquy no fewer than four times and in the discussions that follow these soliloquies he dominates the conversation and the decision-making. Very often, what a character says in a drama (and, in fact, in everyday life), is modified by the presence of other people. (There have been some good examples of this already in this play.) But in soliloquy, Shakespeare's usual practice is to make a person say exactly what he thinks. For a proper understanding of the play, it is essential for the reader or watcher to form an opinion about Brutus and his reasons for wanting to murder Caesar and though the text in this scene is at times rather difficult, it gives a fascinating picture of a great idealist struggling under the weight of an enormous problem. This doesn't mean that he is by any means an entirely admirable person; in fact, we see all too clearly how high principles can go hand in hand with the most foolish errors of judgment, and Brutus's own motives, though almost certainly sincere, seem to show a good deal of self-righteousness and a capacity for self-deception. Nevertheless, it is clear that Brutus's sincerity, his affection for his wife, his kindness to his boy servant and the tremendous admiration and respect that the other conspirators feel for him, are all intended by Shakespeare to make us feel very sympathetic towards him. This fact must be weighed carefully, along with others, in forming opinions about him.

Stage Direction. *orchard:* garden.

1-2. Brutus wants to find out how near daybreak it is but the clouds, associated with the storm, prevent this.

4. 'I wish I could sleep so well.' As he points out later in the scene, he has been awake all night.

5. *When, Lucius, when?* 'When *are* you coming, boy?'

7. *taper:* candle.

ACT TWO

Enter BRUTUS *in his orchard*

Brutus

　What, Lucius, ho!
　I cannot by the progress of the stars
　Give guess how near to day. Lucius, I say!
　I would it were my fault to sleep so soundly.
　When, Lucius, when? Awake, I say! What, Lucius!　　*5*

Enter LUCIUS

Lucius

　Call'd you, my lord?

Brutus

　Get me a taper in my study, Lucius;
　When it is lighted, come and call me here.

Lucius

　I will, my lord.

Exit

10-34. This speech is a problem in that the thought is involved, and Brutus's motives for wanting to murder Caesar seem feeble, considering how little actual evidence of Caesar's tyranny he mentions. The complicated language reflects the anxiety and doubt in Brutus's mind and is a natural consequence of it. Brutus is no doubt strongly influenced by Cassius's arguments, by the anonymous messages that Cassius has planted here and there, and not least by his own family history with its record of dedicated aristocratic service to Rome (lines 53-4). In the end, he convinces himself by arguing that the real danger lies in what Caesar might do, if he is given more power, rather than what he has already done. Is this self-deception or shrewd political insight?

11. *spurn:* kick, strike.

12. *the general:* the good of the people.

14-15. The act of crowning Caesar is here compared with a fine day (an apparently agreeable event) that might make poisonous snakes come out of their lairs (persuade Caesar to use his power viciously), making life dangerous for the unwary walkers (the people of Rome).

15-17. *Crown him—that!* 'If we do that.' Brutus is appalled by the prospect and carries on the metaphor by suggesting that the act of crowning Caesar would not only turn him into a dangerous animal but actually provide him with a 'sting' (give him the means to do harm as well).

18-19. *Th' abuse . . . power:* 'Authority becomes corrupt when it exercises its power without mercy.'

20. *his affections sway'd:* 'his feelings guided (him)'.

22. *lowliness:* a humble manner. He means that an ambitious man frequently puts on such a manner to gain popularity, then casts it off when he has achieved power.

24. *upmost round:* the highest rung.

26. *base degrees:* lowest rungs of the ladder (i.e. the lower positions he occupied on his way up to supreme power).

28. *prevent:* 'let us act to make it impossible.'

28-31. *since the quarrel . . . extremities:* 'since our grievance is unconvincing as it stands, in view of its apparently harmless nature, put it this way: that his present tendencies, if carried further, will lead to various atrocities.' Is this a very impressive argument?

33. *as his kind:* as is the nature of snakes. Note how Brutus's fear of Caesar makes him repeatedly speak of him as though he were a venomous reptile.

35-8. This is obviously one of the messages planted on Brutus by Cassius, or on his orders.

Brutus

It must be by his death; and for my part,   *10*
I know no personal cause to spurn at him,
But for the general: he would be crown'd.
How that might change his nature, there's the
        question.
It is the bright day that brings forth the adder,
And that craves wary walking. Crown him—that!   *15*
And then, I grant, we put a sting in him
That at his will he may do danger with.
Th' abuse of greatness is, when it disjoins
Remorse from power; and to speak truth of Caesar,
I have not known when his affections sway'd   *20*
More than his reason. But 'tis a common proof
That lowliness is young ambition's ladder,
Whereto the climber-upward turns his face;
But when he once attains the upmost round,
He then unto the ladder turns his back,   *25*
Looks in the clouds, scorning the base degrees
By which he did ascend. So Caesar may.
Then, lest he may, prevent. And since the quarrel
Will bear no colour for the thing he is,
Fashion it thus—that what he is, augmented,   *30*
Would run to these and these extremities;
And therefore think him as a serpent's egg,
Which, hatch'd, would as his kind grow mischievous,
And kill him in the shell.

Re-enter LUCIUS

Lucius

The taper burneth in your closet, sir.   *35*
Searching the window for a flint, I found
This paper, thus seal'd up; and I am sure
It did not lie there when I went to bed.

Giving him a letter

44. *exhalations, whizzing in the air:* meteors hissing about.

49. *instigations:* suggestions, provocations.

51. *piece it out:* fill in the missing words.
52. *under one man's awe:* in awe of one man.

54. *The Tarquin.* Brutus refers to the time when one of his ancestors drove out the tyrant from Rome. He feels the time has come for history to be repeated.
55. *redress:* correction of injustices and abuses; reform.
56-8. This is the moment of decision. Brutus is now committed to the murder of Caesar, provided that redress will follow (though this, of course, can't be guaranteed).

59. *March is wasted fifteen days:* the fifteenth day of March has come.

Brutus

Get you to bed again, it is not day.
Is not to-morrow, boy, the ides of March?   40

Lucius

I know not, sir.

Brutus

Look in the calendar, and bring me word.

Lucius

I will, sir.

Exit

Brutus

The exhalations, whizzing in the air,
Give so much light that I may read by them.   45

Opens the letter and reads

'Brutus, thou sleep'st. Awake, and see thyself.
Shall Rome, &c. Speak, strike, redress!
Brutus, thou sleep'st; awake.'
Such instigations have been often dropp'd
Where I have took them up.   50

'Shall Rome, &c.' Thus must I piece it out:
Shall Rome stand under one man's awe? What,
        Rome?
My ancestors did from the streets of Rome
The Tarquin drive, when he was call'd a king.
'Speak, strike, redress!' Am I entreated   55
To speak and strike? O Rome, I make thee promise,
If the redress will follow, thou receivest
Thy full petition at the hand of Brutus!

Re-enter LUCIUS

Lucius

Sir, March is wasted fifteen days.

Knocking within

Brutus

'Tis good. Go to the gate; somebody knocks.   60

Exit LUCIUS

71

61. *whet me against:* rouse my feelings against. (Literally, 'sharpen me up').

63-4. *Between the acting . . . motion:* 'The interval between the decision to do something terrible and the deed itself.'

65. *phantasma:* nightmare.

66-9. This passage expresses the sharp conflict between a man's guardian spirit (the immortal part of him) and his bodily powers, when they cannot agree on a course of action. 'The spirit and body are then in a state of debate or conflict, resulting in turmoil for the man concerned, rather like a rebellion in a nation.' Note what agony of mind Brutus suffers over his decision.

70. *brother:* brother-in-law. Cassius has married Brutus's sister.

73. *hats.* Romans did wear hats of various kinds, but Shakespeare probably has contemporary Elizabethan fashions in mind; certainly these are the hats his actors wore on the stage.

76. *favour:* appearance.

77-85. This is the fourth soliloquy Brutus has delivered since the scene began. Each one has shown him to be in a terrible dilemma about the proposed assassination. In this particular speech he hates the furtive-ness that must accompany the conspiracy but admits reluctantly that without it their hopes of success would be nil.

79. *evils are most free:* evil moves with the greatest freedom.

81. *visage:* face. The plot is thought of as a person with a hideous face that must be kept hidden by darkness.

83-5. 'If the conspiracy tries to make its way without disguise or secrecy, it will be doomed to failure.'

84. *Erebus:* the dark region under the earth through which, according to ancient Roman mythology, the spirits of dead men passed on their way to Hell.

Since Cassius first did whet me against Caesar,
I have not slept.
Between the acting of a dreadful thing
And the first motion, all the interim is
Like a phantasma or a hideous dream.   65
The Genius and the mortal instruments
Are then in council; and the state of man,
Like to a little kingdom, suffers then
The nature of an insurrection.

Re-enter LUCIUS

Lucius
  Sir, 'tis your brother Cassius at the door   70
  Who doth desire to see you.
Brutus   Is he alone?
Lucius
  No, sir, there are moe with him.
Brutus   Do you know them?
Lucius
  No, sir; their hats are pluck'd about their ears
  And half their faces buried in their cloaks,
  That by no means I may discover them   75
  By any mark of favour.
Brutus   Let 'em enter.

Exit LUCIUS

They are the faction. O conspiracy,
Sham'st thou to show thy dang'rous brow by night,
When evils are most free? O, then by day
Where wilt thou find a cavern dark enough   80
To mask thy monstrous visage? Seek none,
    conspiracy;
Hide it in smiles and affability!
For if thou path, thy native semblance on,
Not Erebus itself were dim enough
To hide thee from prevention.   85

86. *we are too bold upon your rest:* 'it is wrong of us to disturb your sleep.'

90. Cassius says that all the conspirators have great respect for Brutus and they all wish he had as much respect for himself. This is an indirect and flattering suggestion that he should finally commit himself to the plot.

98-9. This is a naive question; as if he didn't know! He probably doesn't want to be taken for granted and we must remember that nobody yet knows his final decision.
98. *watchful cares:* 'cares or worries that prevent you from sleeping.'

101-11. This discussion about where the sun rises has nothing to do with the plot except possibly as a symbolic reference to the coming 'dawn' after the darkness of tyranny. But it does show the human tendency to make trivial conversation at moments of nervous tension and it also enables Brutus and Cassius to talk alone, during which we must assume that Brutus gives his formal consent to join the conspiracy.

104. *fret:* make a pattern on.

ACT TWO   SCENE I

Enter the conspirators, CASSIUS, CASCA, DECIUS, CINNA, METELLUS CIMBER, *and* TREBONIUS

Cassius
I think we are too bold upon your rest.
Good morrow, Brutus. Do we trouble you?
Brutus
I have been up this hour, awake all night.
Know I these men that come along with you?
Cassius
Yes, every man of them; and no man here   90
But honours you; and every one doth wish
You had but that opinion of yourself
Which every noble Roman bears of you.
This is Trebonius.
Brutus   He is welcome hither.
Cassius
This, Decius Brutus.
Brutus   He is welcome too.   95
Cassius
This, Casca; this, Cinna;
And this, Metellus Cimber.
Brutus   They are all welcome.
What watchful cares do interpose themselves
Betwixt your eyes and night?
Cassius
Shall I entreat a word?   100

They whisper

Decius
Here lies the east. Doth not the day break here?
Casca
No.
Cinna
O, pardon, sir, it doth; and yon grey lines
That fret the clouds are messengers of day.

107. *growing on:* inclined towards.

108. *Weighing:* considering, taking into account.

114-40. In this speech, Brutus's idealism is shown by his belief that the plotters' motives alone should be strong enough to persuade them to go through with their plan without backsliding or treachery. An oath should not be necessary. Brutus's authority, combined with his idealism, cause the conspirators to make three fatal decisions in this scene.

114. *face:* the troubled expressions of men, caused by Caesar's tyranny.

115. *sufferance:* suffering.

time's abuse: the corruption of that period in Rome.

117. *idle bed:* bed of the lazy man.

118. *high-sighted:* selecting its victims from on high, like a hawk. Caesar is being compared with a falcon that pounces on its prey (as in Act I, Scene i, line 74).

119. *by lottery:* by chance or luck, according to Caesar's mood.

these: the word refers to the conspirators' motives, referred to in lines 114-15.

124. *prick us to redress:* urge us to right the wrongs in Rome.

126. *palter:* hesitate, change our minds.

127. *honesty to honesty engag'd:* promises honestly given and accepted.

129. *cautelous:* crafty or deceitful. Brutus says that the formal process of swearing oaths of loyalty and secrecy is only necessary with men of weak or treacherous character such as those who are so lacking in spirit that they seem to *want* to be trodden on. Note that priests are included; this is because the Roman priest was a fortune-teller rather than a minister of religion in the modern sense.

130. *carrion:* men who are like corpses, barely alive.

133. *even:* unblemished.

134. *insuppressive mettle:* indomitable quality.

135-6. *to think . . . oath:* 'by thinking that either our cause or our plan of action needs to be confirmed by a formal promise.'

Casca

> You shall confess that you are both deceiv'd.   *105*
> Here, as I point my sword, the sun arises;
> Which is a great way growing on the south,
> Weighing the youthful season of the year.
> Some two months hence up higher toward the north
> He first presents his fire; and the high east   *110*
> Stands as the Capitol, directly here.

Brutus

> Give me your hands all over, one by one.

Cassius

> And let us swear our resolution.

Brutus

> No, not an oath. If not the face of men,
> The sufferance of our souls, the time's abuse,   *115*
> If these be motives weak, break off betimes,
> And every man hence to his idle bed.
> So let high-sighted tyranny range on,
> Till each man drop by lottery. But if these,
> As I am sure they do, bear fire enough   *120*
> To kindle cowards, and to steel with valour
> The melting spirits of women, then, countrymen,
> What need we any spur but our own cause
> To prick us to redress? What other bond
> Than secret Romans that have spoke the word   *125*
> And will not palter? And what other oath
> Than honesty to honesty engag'd
> That this shall be or we will fall for it?
> Swear priests and cowards and men cautelous,
> Old feeble carrions and such suffering souls   *130*
> That welcome wrongs; unto bad causes swear
> Such creatures as men doubt; but do not stain
> The even virtue of our enterprise,
> Nor th' insuppressive mettle of our spirits,
> To think that or our cause or our performance   *135*
> Did need an oath; when every drop of blood
> That every Roman bears, and nobly bears,

138. *Is guilty of a several bastardy:* shows that it is not truly Roman and therefore it is despicable. Brutus has pressed home his point at great length. Afterwards, nobody seems inclined to question his opinion.

144. *silver hairs.* Cicero is an elderly man with grey hair, but the word 'silver' also suggests the precious metal. The suggestion is that Cicero's age and the respect in which he is held will 'buy' popularity.

148. *no whit:* not at all.
149. *gravity:* dignity and stability.

150. *break with:* reveal the secret to.

152-3. Would Brutus himself follow anything begun by other men?

153-4. Again, as with the question of taking an oath, Brutus's decision is immediately and unquestioningly accepted. Notice in particular how Casca suddenly changes his mind, after the opinion he expressed in line 143.

155. *well urg'd:* 'a good suggestion.'

158. *a shrewd contriver:* a cunning schemer.
158-60. *his means . . . annoy us all:* 'he has the capacity, if he acts shrewdly and wisely, to harm us all.' Compare Cassius's ruthlessness and realistic sense of danger with Brutus's hopeful idealism.

164: *envy:* malice. Brutus doesn't want the murder to show any signs of spite, and the killing of Antony would lay them open to this accusation.

Is guilty of a several bastardy,
If he do break the smallest particle
Of any promise that hath pass'd from him.   *140*

Cassius

But what of Cicero? Shall we sound him?
I think he will stand very strong with us.

Casca

Let us not leave him out.

Cinna   No, by no means.

Metellus

O, let us have him; for his silver hairs
Will purchase us a good opinion,   *145*
And buy men's voices to commend our deeds.
It shall be said his judgment rul'd our hands;
Our youths and wildness shall no whit appear,
But all be buried in his gravity.

Brutus

O, name him not! Let us not break with him;   *150*
For he will never follow any thing
That other men begin.

Cassius   Then leave him out.

Casca

Indeed he is not fit.

Decius

Shall no man else be touch'd but only Caesar?

Cassius

Decius, well urg'd. I think it is not meet   *155*
Mark Antony, so well belov'd of Caesar,
Should outlive Caesar. We shall find of him
A shrewd contriver; and you know his means,
If he improve them, may well stretch so far
As to annoy us all; which to prevent,   *160*
Let Antony and Caesar fall together.

Brutus

Our course will seem too bloody, Caius Cassius,
To cut the head off and then hack the limbs—
Like wrath in death and envy afterwards;

165. *limb of Caesar:* like a part of his body and therefore useless once Caesar has been killed.

167. Brutus says that it is Caesar's 'spirit' that has to be destroyed and reluctantly admits that the only way to achieve this is by the death of Caesar's body as well.
169. *come by:* get under our control.

171. *gentle:* noble.

173–4. The reference is to the custom, in hunting, of slicing up the carcass of a deer in a ceremonial way, unlike the cruder method of disposing of lesser animals such as the fox. Brutus is desperately trying to make the proposed murder seem less distasteful than it really is.
175–7. *let our . . . chide 'em:* 'let us whip up our passions in order to do the deed and then appear to rebuke ourselves for what we have done, in the same way that cunning masters treat their servants.'
178–9. Brutus thinks this will make the murder appear to be an act of necessity, not prompted by malice.

180. *purgers:* doctors who heal by helping the body to rid itself of harmful substances. Brutus hopes to be regarded as a physician rather than a murderer!

184. *engrafted love:* firmly-rooted affection. Cassius is the only conspirator to stand up to Brutus but after Brutus has interrupted him, he doesn't renew his objection. Later, however, it proves to be a disastrous mistake not to murder Antony as well.

187. *take thought:* give way to despair.
188. *that were much he should:* 'he is hardly likely to do that!' There are several references in the play to Antony's love of a gay life.

190. *no fear:* nothing to fear.

192. Striking clocks were in existence in Shakespeare's day but not in ancient Rome.

For Antony is but a limb of Caesar.   *165*
Let's be sacrificers, but not butchers, Caius.
We all stand up against the spirit of Caesar,
And in the spirit of men there is no blood.
O that we then could come by Caesar's spirit,
And not dismember Caesar! But, alas,   *170*
Caesar must bleed for it! And, gentle friends,
Let's kill him boldly, but not wrathfully;
Let's carve him as a dish fit for the gods,
Not hew him as a carcase fit for hounds;
And let our hearts, as subtle masters do,   *175*
Stir up their servants to an act of rage,
And after seem to chide 'em. This shall make
Our purpose necessary, and not envious;
Which so appearing to the common eyes
We shall be call'd purgers, not murderers.   *180*
And for Mark Antony, think not of him;
For he can do no more than Caesar's arm
When Caesar's head is off.
Cassius   Yet I fear him;
  For in the engrafted love he bears to Caesar—
Brutus
  Alas, good Cassius, do not think of him!   *185*
If he love Caesar, all that he can do
Is to himself take thought and die for Caesar;
And that were much he should, for he is given
To sports, to wildness, and much company.
Trebonius
  There is no fear in him. Let him not die;   *190*
For he will live, and laugh at this hereafter.

Clock strikes

Brutus
  Peace! Count the clock.
Cassius   The clock hath stricken three.
Trebonius
  'Tis time to part.

196-7. 'Contrary to the opinion he once held about imagination, dreams and omens.'

198. *apparent prodigies:* ominous things that have appeared.

200. *augurers:* priests who made predictions after observing ominous events or making sacrifices.

204-6. These are all examples of powerful beasts which can be caught by simple devices, e.g. the unicorn by being tricked into getting its horn stuck in a tree, or the bear by means of a glass (mirror). Decius is sneering at Caesar and saying that he can be tricked equally easily by a flatterer.
205. *holes:* i.e. dug in the ground.
206. *toils:* nets.

210. *give his humour the true bent:* 'twist his mood in the way that suits us.'

214. *uttermost:* latest.

215. *doth bear Caesar hard:* hates Caesar, bears a grudge against Caesar.
216. *rated:* criticized, rebuked.

218. *go along by him:* call on him.

Cassius   But it is doubtful yet
  Whether Caesar will come forth to-day or no;
  For he is superstitious grown of late,   195
  Quite from the main opinion he held once
  Of fantasy, of dreams, and ceremonies.
  It may be these apparent prodigies,
  The unaccustom'd terror of this night,
  And the persuasion of his augurers,   200
  May hold him from the Capitol to-day.

Decius
  Never fear that. If he be so resolv'd,
  I can o'ersway him; for he loves to hear
  That unicorns may be betray'd with trees,
  And bears with glasses, elephants with holes,   205
  Lions with toils, and men with flatterers;
  But when I tell him he hates flatterers,
  He says he does, being then most flattered.
  Let me work;
  For I can give his humour the true bent,   210
  And I will bring him to the Capitol.

Cassius
  Nay, we will all of us be there to fetch him.

Brutus
  By the eighth hour. Is that the uttermost?

Cinna
  Be that the uttermost, and fail not then.

Metellus
  Caius Ligarius doth bear Caesar hard,   215
  Who rated him for speaking well of Pompey.
  I wonder none of you have thought of him.

Brutus
  Now, good Metellus, go along by him.
  He loves me well, and I have given him reasons;
  Send him but hither, and I'll fashion him.   220

Cassius
  The morning comes upon's. We'll leave you, Brutus.
  And, friends, disperse yourselves; but all remember

223. *true Romans:* loyal and determined citizens of Rome.

225. 'Don't let our faces betray our plans.'

226-7. He says that they should bear their responsibilities with no appearance of strain.

230. *honey-heavy dew.* This conveys the comforting and refreshing quality of deep sleep.

231. *figures and fantasies:* mental impressions and products of a warped imagination, caused by anxiety. As at the beginning of the scene, Brutus is envious of the boy's happy and innocent state of mind which enables him to sleep so soundly.

237-309. In this glimpse into Brutus's private life, compare his attitude towards Portia with that of Caesar towards Calphurnia.

237. *ungently:* discourteously.

240. *arms across:* either folded, or clasped round the shoulders. This seems to have been the typical posture of a person suffering from anxiety or depression.

246. *wafture:* wave, gesture.

248-50. 'Not wishing to increase your irritation, which already seemed intense, and hoping that it was just the result of a passing mood.'

What you have said, and show yourselves true
   Romans.

Brutus

Good gentlemen, look fresh and merrily;
Let not our looks put on our purposes,   225
But bear it as our Roman actors do,
With untir'd spirits and formal constancy.
And so good morrow to you every one.

Exeunt all but BRUTUS

Boy! Lucius! Fast asleep? It is no matter;
Enjoy the honey-heavy dew of slumber.   230
Thou hast no figures nor no fantasies
Which busy care draws in the brains of men;
Therefore thou sleep'st so sound.

Enter PORTIA

Portia   Brutus, my lord!

Brutus

Portia, what mean you? Wherefore rise you now?
It is not for your health thus to commit   235
Your weak condition to the raw cold morning.

Portia

Nor for yours neither. Y'have ungently, Brutus,
Stole from my bed; and yesternight at supper
You suddenly arose and walk'd about,
Musing and sighing, with your arms across;   240
And when I ask'd you what the matter was,
You star'd upon me with ungentle looks.
I urg'd you further; then you scratch'd your head
And too impatiently stamp'd with your foot.
Yet I insisted; yet you answer'd not,   245
But with an angry wafture of your hand
Gave sign for me to leave you. So I did,
Fearing to strengthen that impatience
Which seem'd too much enkindled; and withal
Hoping it was but an effect of humour,   250
Which sometime hath his hour with every man.

253-5. Portia means that if her husband's anxiety had changed his appearance as much as it had changed his behaviour, she would not be able to recognize him.

259. *embrace the means:* take the necessary steps.

261. *physical:* healthy.

262. *unbraced:* with his doublet (coat) unbuttoned.
suck up the humours: breathe in the damp mist, that was believed to be particularly unhealthy.

265. *vile contagion:* poisonous vapour.

266. *rheumy and unpurged air:* damp air, unpurified by the warmth of the sun.

268. Portia rightly diagnoses the trouble as something in Brutus's mind, not some physical ailment, as he has tried to explain.

271. *charm:* beg.

273. *incorporate:* 'make one body'. Shakespeare makes Portia speak in terms of the Christian marriage service.
274. *your half.* This expresses the idea (still common today) that one's marriage partner is one's other or 'better' half.
275. *heavy:* dejected.

278-80. *gentle.* The word here means 'kind'. Portia says that her kneeling would not be necessary if Brutus would only be kind to her.
281-2. *Is it excepted ... to you?:* 'Am I not allowed to know any secrets that concern you?'

It will not let you eat, nor talk, nor sleep;
And, could it work so much upon your shape
As it hath much prevail'd on your condition,
I should not know you Brutus. Dear my lord,   *255*
Make me acquainted with your cause of grief.
Brutus
I am not well in health, and that is all.
Portia
Brutus is wise, and, were he not in health,
He would embrace the means to come by it.
Brutus
Why, so I do. Good Portia, go to bed.   *260*
Portia
Is Brutus sick, and is it physical
To walk unbraced and suck up the humours
Of the dank morning? What, is Brutus sick,
And will he steal out of his wholesome bed,
To dare the vile contagion of the night,   *265*
And tempt the rheumy and unpurged air
To add unto his sickness? No, my Brutus;
You have some sick offence within your mind,
Which by the right and virtue of my place
I ought to know of; and upon my knees   *270*
I charm you, by my once-commended beauty,
By all your vows of love, and that great vow
Which did incorporate and make us one,
That you unfold to me, your self, your half,
Why you are heavy—and what men to-night   *275*
Have had resort to you; for here have been
Some six or seven, who did hide their faces
Even from darkness.
Brutus   Kneel not, gentle Portia.
Portia
I should not need, if you were gentle Brutus.
Within the bond of marriage, tell me, Brutus,   *280*
Is it excepted I should know no secrets
That appertain to you? Am I your self

283. *But . . . or limitation:* 'Only in a certain way or for a limited period.' These are legal terms, and Portia is deliberately suggesting that Brutus is acting legalistically, not lovingly.

285-8. Portia is trying to touch her husband's conscience by suggesting that if he will not confide in her, she might as well be his whore rather than his wife. London prostitutes in Shakespeare's day lived mainly in the suburbs of the city, thus the word 'suburbs' suggests (1) that Portia is only 'on the fringe' of Brutus's affection and (2) that he is using her for sexual pleasure only.

289-90. *ruddy drops . . . heart:* 'blood that goes to and from my heavy heart'.

295. *Cato's daughter.* Portia's father was a determined enemy of Caesar and a man of great integrity, so she has reason to be proud of her parentage.
296. *no stronger than my sex:* no stronger than any other woman.

299. *strong proof of my constancy:* severe test of my determination.

303-6. It seems that Portia has won over Brutus but, since the details of the conspiracy have already been revealed, there is no need for the audience to hear them again, so Shakespeare puts in a timely interruption (the knocking). Portia's nervous behaviour later (Act II, Scene iv) shows that Brutus does, in fact, tell her everything.

308. 'The full explanation of the worry-lines on my forehead.'

But, as it were, in sort or limitation?
To keep with you at meals, comfort your bed,
And talk to you sometimes? Dwell I but in the
    suburbs   *285*
Of your good pleasure? If it be no more,
Portia is Brutus' harlot, not his wife.

Brutus

You are my true and honourable wife,
As dear to me as are the ruddy drops
That visit my sad heart.   *290*

Portia

If this were true, then should I know this secret.
I grant I am a woman; but withal
A woman that Lord Brutus took to wife.
I grant I am a woman; but withal
A woman well reputed, Cato's daughter.   *295*
Think you I am no stronger than my sex,
Being so father'd and so husbanded?
Tell me your counsels, I will not disclose 'em.
I have made strong proof of my constancy,
Giving myself a voluntary wound   *300*
Here, in the thigh. Can I bear that with patience,
And not my husband's secrets?

Brutus   O ye gods,
Render me worthy of this noble wife!

          Knocking within

Hark, hark! one knocks. Portia, go in awhile,
And by and by thy bosom shall partake   *305*
The secrets of my heart.
All my engagements I will construe to thee,
All the charactery of my sad brows.
Leave me with haste.

          Exit PORTIA

          Lucius, who's that knocks?

        Enter LUCIUS *and* LIGARIUS

311. Metellus suggested bringing Caius Ligarius into the conspiracy (Act II, Scene i, lines 215-17).

312. *How?* 'How are you?'

313. *Vouchsafe:* please accept.

315. *wear a kerchief.* It was usual, in Elizabethan England, for sick people to wear a strip of cloth round their heads in public. This was intended to give them some protection, e.g. from the jostling by the crowd, or at least to indicate that the wearer was ill.

321. He now takes off the 'kerchief' to demonstrate his regained health. *Soul of Rome!* A striking phrase, showing once again the way in which many people looked up to and depended on Brutus in their movement against Caesar.

322. This is a reference to Brutus's noble ancestry.

323-4. *Thou, like an exorcist . . . spirit.* An exorcist was a person who could control spirits, usually by calling them up from the underworld. Ligarius means that Brutus has put new life into his previously dead (*mortified*) hopes for Rome.

328-9. There is a good deal of play on the significance of sickness or illness in this part of the scene and also elsewhere in the play. Generally, physical ill-health represents some deeper personal or social disorder. Here, the two characters understand one another easily. Caesar's 'illness' (death) will bring 'health' (new life) to others.

330-1. *as we are . . . must be done:* 'as we are on the way to the person who must receive our "treatment".'

332. *new-fir'd:* re-kindled, like a fire. Note the blind devotion that Brutus can inspire. To conclude a scene that has been full of discussion,

Lucius

  Here is a sick man that would speak with you.   *310*

Brutus

  Caius Ligarius, that Metellus spake of.

  Boy, stand aside. Caius Ligarius, how?

Ligarius

  Vouchsafe good morrow from a feeble tongue.

Brutus

  O, what a time have you chose out, brave Caius,

  To wear a kerchief! Would you were not sick!   *315*

Ligarius

  I am not sick, if Brutus have in hand

  Any exploit worthy the name of honour.

Brutus

  Such an exploit have I in hand, Ligarius,

  Had you a healthful ear to hear of it.

Ligarius

  By all the gods that Romans bow before,   *320*

  I here discard my sickness.

Pulls off his kerchief

                  Soul of Rome!

  Brave son, deriv'd from honourable loins!

  Thou, like an exorcist, hast conjur'd up

  My mortified spirit. Now bid me run,

  And I will strive with things impossible;   *325*

  Yea, get the better of them. What's to do?

Brutus

  A piece of work that will make sick men whole.

Ligarius

  But are not some whole that we must make sick?

Brutus

  That must we also. What it is, my Caius,

  I shall unfold to thee, as we are going,   *330*

  To whom it must be done.

Ligarius   Set on your foot,

  And with a heart new-fir'd I follow you

with very little action, Shakespeare ends on a note of keen anticipation of future events.

SCENE II

The storm, and all the superstition associated with it, is now presented from the point of view of Caesar and Calphurnia. The fact that husband and wife disagree is not so important as the question whether events will persuade Caesar to go to the Capitol for the crowning ceremony, or not. A large part of this scene is also open to some very varied interpretations. Is Caesar really afraid, superstitious, pompous and susceptible to flattery? Does he waver and show indecision? Few, if any, of the answers to these questions can be proved conclusively but the reader must draw some conclusions of his own if he is to appreciate the play properly. One fact, though, is fairly obvious, and that is Caesar's evident generosity at the end of the scene. This shows him at his best and the conspirators at their hypocritical worst, as Brutus is painfully aware.

5. *present:* immediate.

6. *success:* outcome or result.

10-12. This example of Caesar's arrogance is even more remarkable than others in that he hasn't even the excuse that there is an audience of Romans to impress.

13. *stood on ceremonies:* 'took much notice of omens.'

14-16. *There is one . . . watch:* 'Somebody within this house has reported

To do I know not what; but it sufficeth
That Brutus leads me on.

Thunder

Brutus   Follow me, then.

Exeunt

SCENE II—*Rome. Caesar's house*

Thunder and lightning. Enter JULIUS CAESAR *in his
night-gown*

Caesar
Nor heaven nor earth have been at peace to-night.
Thrice hath Calphurnia in her sleep cried out
'Help, ho! They murder Caesar!' Who's within?

Enter a SERVANT

Servant
My lord?
Caesar
Go bid the priests do present sacrifice,   5
And bring me their opinions of success.
Servant
I will, my lord.

Exit. Enter CALPHURNIA

Calphurnia
What mean you, Caesar? Think you to walk forth?
You shall not stir out of your house to-day.
Caesar
Caesar shall forth; the things that threaten'd me   10
Ne'er look'd but on my back. When they shall see
The face of Caesar, they are vanished.
Calphurnia
Caesar, I never stood on ceremonies,
Yet now they fright me. There is one within,

93

that the city's watchmen have seen some frightful sights, quite apart from what we have experienced ourselves.'

17. *whelped:* given birth to cubs.

18. *yawn'd:* opened wide.

20. *right form of war:* proper order of battle.

21. *which:* refers to *clouds* in line 19.

22. *hurtled:* sounded loudly; clashed.

25. *beyond all use:* utterly unnatural.

26-31. Caesar justifies himself by saying that bad omens apply to everybody, but Calphurnia expresses the more general view of the Elizabethans by saying that they refer especially to people at the top of the social scale. Shakespeare himself certainly uses portents in this way in a number of his plays and the danger to Caesar is something that a contemporary audience would be aware of at once.

32-3. 'Cowardly men suffer all the agony of dying, in their imagination, many times before their actual deaths; brave men have to face this ordeal only once.'

34-7. It is difficult to say whether this fatalistic view of death is genuine or just another part of Caesar's act of bravado. We must be on our guard not to regard *all* Caesar's words and ideas as false and pompous.

37. *augurers:* see Act II, Scene i, line 200.

39. *offering:* an animal offered for sacrifice.

40. *heart.* In Shakespeare's day, this vital organ was associated with courage. Its absence would be regarded as a very bad omen.

41. 'The gods have made this occur in order to shame cowardly men.'

Besides the things that we have heard and seen,   *15*
Recounts most horrid sights seen by the watch.
A lioness hath whelped in the streets,
And graves have yawn'd and yielded up their dead;
Fierce fiery warriors fight upon the clouds,
In ranks and squadrons and right form of war,   *20*
Which drizzled blood upon the Capitol;
The noise of battle hurtled in the air;
Horses did neigh, and dying men did groan,
And ghosts did shriek and squeal about the streets.
O Caesar, these things are beyond all use,   *25*
And I do fear them!

Caesar   What can be avoided,
Whose end is purpos'd by the mighty gods?
Yet Caesar shall go forth; for these predictions
Are to the world in general as to Caesar.

Calphurnia
When beggars die there are no comets seen: *30*
The heavens themselves blaze forth the death of
      princes.

Caesar
Cowards die many times before their deaths:
The valiant never taste of death but once.
Of all the wonders that I yet have heard,
It seems to me most strange that men should fear,   *35*
Seeing that death, a necessary end,
Will come when it will come.

Re-enter SERVANT

                What say the augurers?

Servant
They would not have you to stir forth to-day.
Plucking the entrails of an offering forth,
They could not find a heart within the beast.   *40*

Caesar
The gods do this in shame of cowardice.
Caesar should be a beast without a heart,

44-8. Caesar makes the incredible claim that he and danger are like twin brothers, but that he himself is the more powerful of the two.

49. 'Your common-sense is overwhelmed by complacency.'

56. *for thy humour:* to satisfy your fancy.

60. *in very happy time:* at just the right time.

63. Though Caesar has agreed that he should be reported to the Senate as sick (line 55), he will not allow Decius to do this as Decius can see for himself that Caesar is perfectly well. A more intimate friend, such as Antony, might have been permitted to convey the lie.

67. *greybeards:* foolish old men.

If he should stay at home to-day for fear.
No, Caesar shall not. Danger knows full well
That Caesar is more dangerous than he: *45*
We are two lions litter'd in one day,
And I the elder and more terrible;
And Caesar shall go forth.

Calphurnia   Alas, my lord,
Your wisdom is consum'd in confidence.
Do not go forth to-day. Call it my fear   *50*
That keeps you in the house, and not your own.
We'll send Mark Antony to the Senate House,
And he shall say you are not well to-day.
Let me, upon my knee, prevail in this.

Caesar
Mark Antony shall say I am not well;   *55*
And for thy humour I will stay at home.

Enter DECIUS

Here's Decius Brutus, he shall tell them so.

Decius
Caesar, all hail! Good morrow, worthy Caesar.
I come to fetch you to the Senate House.

Caesar
And you are come in very happy time,   *60*
To bear my greeting to the senators
And tell them that I will not come to-day.
Cannot, is false; and that I dare not, falser;
I will not come to-day. Tell them so, Decius.

Calphurnia
Say he is sick.

Caesar   Shall Caesar send a lie?   *65*
Have I in conquest stretch'd mine arm so far,
To be afeard to tell greybeards the truth?
Decius, go tell them Caesar will not come.

Decius
Most mighty Caesar, let me know some cause,
Lest I be laugh'd at when I tell them so.   *70*

75. *stays me:* keeps or detains me.
76. *to-night:* last night.
statua: statue.

80. *apply for :* interpret as.

83. *all amiss:* quite wrongly.

89. The four vital words in this line all mean much the same and refer to the Christian belief (which developed, of course, long after Caesar's time) in the protective value of 'relics' such as pieces of clothing stained with the blood of martyrs, or the bones of saints. Decius says the dream means that Romans would try to obtain similar relics from Caesar's blood, believing that they would provide special protection or just be valuable souvenirs that others would envy.
91. Caesar is immediately deceived by Decius's flattery, exactly as Decius predicted (Act II, Scene i, lines 202-11).
93. *concluded:* decided.

96-7. *a mock ... to say:* 'someone is likely to ridicule you by saying.'

101. We have already seen how sensitive Caesar is to the idea that he might be afraid of anything. Decius is fully aware of this weakness and exploits it effectively here. We can imagine Caesar's angry frown at this point, making Decius hasten to add some more soothing words. **103.** *proceeding:* progress, advancement.

Caesar

    The cause is in my will: I will not come.
    That is enough to satisfy the Senate.
    But for your private satisfaction,
    Because I love you, I will let you know:
    Calphurnia here, my wife, stays me at home.   *75*
    She dreamt to-night she saw my statua,
    Which, like a fountain with an hundred spouts,
    Did run pure blood; and many lusty Romans
    Came smiling and did bathe their hands in it.
    And these does she apply for warnings and portents   *80*
    And evils imminent, and on her knee
    Hath begg'd that I will stay at home to-day.

Decius

    This dream is all amiss interpreted;
    It was a vision fair and fortunate.
    Your statue spouting blood in many pipes,   *85*
    In which so many smiling Romans bath'd,
    Signifies that from you great Rome shall suck
    Reviving blood, and that great men shall press
    For tinctures, stains, relics, and cognizance.
    This by Calphurnia's dream is signified.   *90*

Caesar

    And this way have you well expounded it.

Decius

    I have, when you have heard what I can say—
    And know it now: the Senate have concluded
    To give this day a crown to mighty Caesar.
    If you shall send them word you will not come,   *95*
    Their minds may change. Besides, it were a mock
    Apt to be render'd, for some one to say
    'Break up the Senate till another time,
    When Caesar's wife shall meet with better dreams'.
    If Caesar hide himself, shall they not whisper   *100*
    'Lo, Caesar is afraid'?
    Pardon me, Caesar; for my dear dear love
    To your proceeding bids me tell you this,

104. 'Reason must be ruled by my affection for you.'

107. This is the second time in this scene that Caesar's mind has been changed for him.

108-13. The rest of the conspirators now arrive to escort Caesar to the Capitol, as agreed in Act II, Scene i, line 212. Here, Caesar greets them courteously and shows himself to be kind and considerate. This is a good example of dramatic irony since everybody present (including the audience) knows what is in store for him, while Caesar himself does not.

116-17. *Antony . . . notwithstanding up:* 'Antony, who spends long hours at night drinking and making merry, is already up in spite of this.'

119. 'I am at fault for causing you to wait for me.'

120-3. Caesar's kind greetings continue as the others arrive. Note that Cassius is not included amongst those who call for Caesar. Perhaps his more obvious and intense dislike for Caesar would spoil the friendly atmosphere, and the conspirators want to lull Caesar into a sense of security.

126-7. The repetition of *friends* and the offer of *wine* add to the irony of the situation.

And reason to my love is liable.
Caesar
How foolish do your fears seem now, Calphurnia!   *105*
I am ashamed I did yield to them.
Give me my robe, for I will go.

    Enter BRUTUS, LIGARIUS, METELLUS, CASCA,
        TREBONIUS, CINNA, *and* PUBLIUS

And look where Publius is come to fetch me.
Publius
Good morrow, Caesar.
Caesar   Welcome, Publius.
What, Brutus, are you stirr'd so early too?   *110*
Good morrow, Casca. Caius Ligarius,
Caesar was ne'er so much your enemy
As that same ague which hath made you lean.
What is't o'clock?
Brutus   Caesar, 'tis strucken eight.
Caesar
I thank you for your pains and courtesy.   *115*

        Enter ANTONY

See! Antony, that revels long o' nights,
Is notwithstanding up. Good morrow, Antony.
Antony
So to most noble Caesar.
Caesar   Bid them prepare within.
I am to blame to be thus waited for.
Now, Cinna. Now, Metellus. What, Trebonius!   *120*
I have an hour's talk in store for you.
Remember that you call on me to-day;
Be near me, that I may remember you.
Trebonius
Caesar, I will. [*Aside*] And so near will I be,
That your best friends shall wish I had been further. *125*
Caesar
Good friends, go in and taste some wine with me;

101

128-9. 'It grieves me to think that being *like* friends and being *true* friends are not the same thing.' Shakespeare doesn't want us to feel that Brutus is quite as treacherous and cold-blooded as the others.

SCENE III

Tension rises as we hear that the conspiracy is known by at least one friend of Caesar. Has one of the conspirators taken advantage of Brutus's refusal to bind them all by an oath? More important, will the whole plot be revealed?

1-5. Artemidorus lists the conspirators in their order of importance in the play.

7. *Security gives way to conspiracy:* 'Your mistaken sense of security gives conspiracy its opportunity.'

10. *suitor:* a person who makes a petition or request. It was usual for suitors to present their requests to rulers on special occasions arranged for the purpose. Later (Act III, Scene i, line 11), Artemidorus is rebuked by Caesar for presenting his petition in the wrong place.

11-12. *virtue . . . emulation :* 'greatness cannot exist unharmed by the envy of others.'

14. *contrive:* plot.

SCENE IV

Portia's agitation is proof that her husband did, in fact, tell her all about the conspiracy as he promised in Act II, Scene i, lines 305-6. Her intense nervousness serves both to raise the tension in the theatre and show how deeply she is involved in her husband's affairs.

And we, like friends, will straightway go together.
Brutus [*Aside*]
That every like is not the same, O Caesar,
The heart of Brutus earns to think upon!

Exeunt

SCENE III—*Rome. A street near the Capitol*
                Enter ARTEMIDORUS *reading a paper*

Artemidorus
'Caesar, beware of Brutus; take heed of Cassius;
come not near Casca; have an eye to Cinna; trust
not Trebonius; mark well Metellus Cimber; Decius
Brutus loves thee not; thou hast wrong'd Caius
Ligarius. There is but one mind in all these men, and   5
it is bent against Caesar. If thou beest not immortal,
look about you. Security gives way to conspiracy.
The mighty gods defend thee!
                                    Thy lover,
                                          ARTEMIDORUS.'
Here will I stand till Caesar pass along,
And as a suitor will I give him this.   10
My heart laments that virtue cannot live
Out of the teeth of emulation.
If thou read this, O Caesar, thou mayest live;
If not, the fates with traitors do contrive.

Exit

SCENE IV—*Rome. Before the house of Brutus*

Enter PORTIA *and* LUCIUS

Portia
I prithee, boy, run to the Senate House.
Stay not to answer me, but get thee gone.
Why dost thou stay?

6. *constancy:* self-control.

7. Portia is afraid that she will blurt out more than she should and thus betray Brutus. The *huge mountain* is to prevent her mouth expressing what her heart feels.

9. *keep counsel:* keep a secret.

13-14. This, of course, is a mere excuse, as Brutus was quite well, physically, when he left.

18. *bustling rumour:* confused and riotous noise. This is just Portia's imagination, resulting from her agitation.

Lucius   To know my errand, madam.

Portia

I would have had thee there and here again,
Ere I can tell thee what thou shouldst do there.   5
[*Aside*] O constancy, be strong upon my side!
Set a huge mountain 'tween my heart and tongue!
I have a man's mind, but a woman's might.
How hard it is for women to keep counsel!—
Art thou here yet?

Lucius   Madam, what should I do?   10
Run to the Capitol, and nothing else?
And so return to you, and nothing else?

Portia

Yes, bring me word, boy, if thy lord look well,
For he went sickly forth; and take good note
What Caesar doth, what suitors press to him.   15
Hark, boy! What noise is that?

Lucius

I hear none, madam.

Portia   Prithee listen well.

I heard a bustling rumour, like a fray,
And the wind brings it from the Capitol.

Lucius

Sooth, madam, I hear nothing.

Enter the SOOTHSAYER

Portia   Come hither, fellow.   20

Which way hast thou been?

Soothsayer   At mine own house,
     good lady.

Portia

What is't o'clock?

Soothsayer   About the ninth hour, lady.

Portia

Is Caesar yet gone to the Capitol?

Soothsayer

Madam, not yet. I go to take my stand,

26-8. The *suit* (request) is really no more than a further warning about the Ides of March, originally given in Act I, Scene ii, line 19 and repeated in Act III, Scene i, line 2.

34. *praetors:* see Act I, Scene iii, line 143.

36. *more void:* less crowded.

40. 'May the gods help you in your exploit '(to murder Caesar).

41-2. *Brutus hath . . . not grant.* This is said aloud in an attempt to give some explanation to the boy of what he must have overheard.

44. *merry:* in good spirits.

To see him pass on to the Capitol.   25

Portia

Thou hast some suit to Caesar, hast thou not?

Soothsayer

That I have, lady. If it will please Caesar

To be so good to Caesar as to hear me,

I shall beseech him to befriend himself.

Portia

Why, know'st thou any harm's intended towards

   him?   30

Soothsayer

None that I know will be, much that I fear may chance.

Good morrow to you. Here the street is narrow;

The throng that follows Caesar at the heels,

Of senators, of praetors, common suitors,

Will crowd a feeble man almost to death.   35

I'll get me to a place more void, and there

Speak to great Caesar as he comes along.

Exit

Portia

I must go in. [*Aside*] Ay me, how weak a thing

The heart of woman is! O Brutus,

The heavens speed thee in thine enterprise!   40

Sure the boy heard me.—Brutus hath a suit

That Caesar will not grant.—O, I grow faint.—

Run, Lucius, and commend me to my lord;

Say I am merry. Come to me again,

And bring me word what he doth say to thee.   45

Exeunt severally

The conspiracy has been established, its members agreed upon, its aims decided; only the deed itself remains to be done. So far, Shakespeare has not given us a very favourable picture of Caesar and has presented Brutus as a noble, if misguided, idealist, torn by conflicting loyalties. The effect of all this has been to incline our sympathy towards the conspiracy and cushion the audience against the shock of the murder itself. Now, when the very minutes of Caesar's life are numbered, our sympathy is tilted a little more sharply against the 'tyrant' who, in his last moments, speaks and acts with immense pride. However, the very last moment of all (*Et tu, Brute?—Then fall, Caesar!*) may well produce a different effect.

The situation that follows is one of complete confusion. Some conspirators are triumphant, some afraid of the immediate consequences; all are agitated and talk hurriedly and even aimlessly, joking about the event in their nervous sense of relief. The effect on others is one of complete bewilderment. It is Antony who makes us see exactly what has been done and corrects the balance of our impressions. Brutus wished to 'sacrifice' Caesar and the washing in Caesar's blood, if properly presented on the stage, should resemble one of the most solemn moments in a religious service, for that is how Brutus sees it. He rejected a murder by 'butchers' (Act II, Scene i, line 166) but Antony uses this very word to describe Brutus and his colleagues in his address to the body of Caesar. By the end of the scene it is clear that the conspirators have reached their peak of success and we are left in no doubt that they have a formidable rival who will stop at nothing to avenge Caesar's death.

3. *schedule:* paper, document.

4-5. Trebonius seems to have no request to make but Decius Brutus is no doubt anxious for nobody except the conspirators to surround Caesar and he might have made this up as an excuse just to distract attention from Antony.

7. *touches Caesar nearer:* concerns Caesar more directly.

8. 'Matters that concern me personally will be dealt with last of all.' Though this sounds very generous and impressive, it effectively condemns Caesar to death; a less dramatic display of self-denial might have saved him, since it would have enabled him to read Artemidorus's letter in time to be warned of the danger.

9. Artemidorus's anxiety makes him disrespectful and thereby ruins his chance of saving Caesar.

ACT THREE

Flourish. Enter CAESAR, BRUTUS, CASSIUS, CASCA, DECIUS, METELLUS, TREBONIUS, CINNA, ANTONY, LEPIDUS, ARTEMIDORUS, POPILIUS, PUBLIUS, *and the* SOOTHSAYER

Caesar
  The ides of March are come.
Soothsayer
  Ay, Caesar, but not gone.
Artemidorus
  Hail, Caesar! Read this schedule.
Decius
  Trebonius doth desire you to o'er-read,
  At your best leisure, this his humble suit.   5
Artemidorus
  O Caesar, read mine first; for mine's a suit
  That touches Caesar nearer. Read it, great Caesar.
Caesar
  What touches us ourself shall be last serv'd.
Artemidorus
  Delay not, Caesar; read it instantly.
Caesar
  What, is the fellow mad?
Publius   Sirrah, give place.   10
Cassius
  What, urge you your petitions in the street?
  Come to the Capitol.

          CAESAR *enters the Capitol, the rest following*

13-15. This mysterious hint from Popilius Lena helps to raise the tension sharply at this point. Caesar's death is by no means certain yet.

18. *makes to:* goes towards.

19. *be sudden . . . prevention:* 'be quick or we shall be frustrated.'

21. *turn back:* return alive.

22. At this crucial moment, Cassius's mind turns immediately to suicide, as it so often does in moments of stress.
be constant: 'keep cool.' Brutus controls himself and others better than Cassius does.

25. *knows his time:* 'knows what he has to do. This is to draw aside Antony, Caesar's most loyal and powerful supporter, from the immediate scene of the murder.

28. *presently prefer his suit:* 'present his petition immediately.'

29. *address'd:* prepared.
second. It was usual for petitioners to be supported by friends, known as 'seconds'.

31-2. As in line 8 and elsewhere, Caesar speaks in the third person, which would normally be done only by the monarch, at least in Shakespeare's time. This again emphasizes his pride.

Popilius
  I wish your enterprise to-day may thrive.
Cassius
  What enterprise, Popilius?
Popilius   Fare you well.

Advances to CAESAR

Brutus
  What said Popilius Lena?   15
Cassius
  He wish'd to-day our enterprise might thrive.
  I fear our purpose is discovered.
Brutus
  Look how he makes to Caesar. Mark him.
Cassius
  Casca, be sudden, for we fear prevention.
  Brutus, what shall be done? If this be known,   20
  Cassius or Caesar never shall turn back,
  For I will slay myself.
Brutus   Cassius, be constant.
  Popilius Lena speaks not of our purposes;
  For look, he smiles, and Caesar doth not change.
Cassius
  Trebonius knows his time; for look you, Brutus,   25
  He draws Mark Antony out of the way.

Exeunt ANTONY *and* TREBONIUS

Decius
  Where is Metellus Cimber? Let him go
  And presently prefer his suit to Caesar.
Brutus
  He is address'd; press near and second him.
Cinna
  Casca, you are the first that rears your hand.   30
Caesar
  Are we all ready? What is now amiss
  That Caesar and his Senate must redress?

111

33. *puissant:* powerful.

36. *couchings and courtesies:* grovelling and humble bowing.

37-9. *Might fire . . . children:* 'Might stir the emotions of ordinary men and change fundamental laws into something childish.'
39-43. *Be not fond . . . spaniel fawning:* 'Don't be so foolish as to imagine that Caesar is so unstable that he can be changed from his real nature by methods that make an impression on fools; I mean flattery, bowing low to the ground, and vile, dog-like cringing.'

46. *spurn thee like a cur:* 'kick you out of the way like a dog.' Perhaps at this point Caesar is meant to thrust away Metellus Cimber with his foot.
47-8. Caesar is probably referring to the immediate cause of Metellus Cimber's request (the banishment of his brother) and is saying, 'I have not wronged him, nor will I change my decision without good reason.'

51. *repealing:* recalling from banishment.

54. *freedom of repeal:* the right to return from banishment.

57. *enfranchisement.* This means much the same as *repeal.*

58-9. 'If I were like you, I could easily be influenced by you. If I could beg others to change their minds, your pleading would make me change mine.'
60. *northern star:* pole star, which remains fixed in relation to others and is therefore 'constant'.

Metellus

  Most high, most mighty, and most puissant Caesar,
  Metellus Cimber throws before thy seat
  An humble heart.

Kneeling

Caesar   I must prevent thee, Cimber.   *35*
  These couchings and these lowly courtesies
  Might fire the blood of ordinary men,
  And turn pre-ordinance and first decree
  Into the law of children. Be not fond
  To think that Caesar bears such rebel blood   *40*
  That will be thaw'd from the true quality
  With that which melteth fools—I mean, sweet words,
  Low-crooked curtsies, and base spaniel fawning.
  Thy brother by decree is banished;
  If thou dost bend, and pray, and fawn for him,   *45*
  I spurn thee like a cur out of my way.
  Know, Caesar doth not wrong; nor without cause
  Will he be satisfied.

Metellus

  Is there no voice more worthy than my own
  To sound more sweetly in great Caesar's ear   *50*
  For the repealing of my banish'd brother?

Brutus

  I kiss thy hand, but not in flattery, Caesar,
  Desiring thee that Publius Cimber may
  Have an immediate freedom of repeal.

Caesar

  What, Brutus!

Cassius   Pardon, Caesar! Caesar, pardon!   *55*
  As low as to thy foot doth Cassius fall,
  To beg enfranchisement for Publius Cimber.

Caesar

  I could be well mov'd, if I were as you;
  If I could pray to move, prayers would move me;
  But I am constant as the northern star,   *60*

61-2. 'For the absolutely unmoving and unchanging quality of which there is no equal in the heavens.'

63. *unnumber'd sparks:* 'uncountable numbers of stars.'

66. *furnish'd well:* fully populated.

67. *apprehensive:* able to reason.

69-70. *That unassailable . . . motion:* 'Who stands immovably in his position, unaffected by any disturbance.'

74. *Olympus:* a mountain, supposed by the Romans to be the place where the gods lived. Caesar compares himself with something vast in size and divine in quality. His arrogance has never reached such heights and it is clearly Shakespeare's intention that it should do so just before his death, thus reducing to some extent the impression of brutality that the murder must give.

75. *bootless:* uselessly, in vain.

76. Casca's comment means, in effect, 'Words are useless; a dagger-thrust is more effective.'

77. *Et tu Brute?:* 'You too, Brutus?' An expression of amazement on Caesar's part that one of his best friends should stab him. The use of the Latin words here adds to the drama and pathos of Caesar's death, and from this moment onwards the presentation of Caesar's character undergoes considerable change. When he is dead, all his human weaknesses, physical and temperamental, are forgotten.

80. *pulpits:* platforms for speech-making.

81. *enfranchisement.* Here, this word has much the same meaning as 'liberty' or 'freedom'.

82. There is general panic and confusion, which Brutus tries to calm down.

83. *Ambition's debt is paid:* 'Caesar's ambition has had its reward.' He means that accounts have been settled and that nobody else will be hurt.

Of whose true-fix'd and resting quality
There is no fellow in the firmament.
The skies are painted with unnumber'd sparks,
They are all fire, and every one doth shine;
But there's but one in all doth hold his place.   65
So in the world: 'tis furnish'd well with men,
And men are flesh and blood, and apprehensive;
Yet in the number I do know but one
That unassailable holds on his rank,
Unshak'd of motion; and that I am he,   70
Let me a little show it, even in this—
That I was constant Cimber should be banish'd,
And constant do remain to keep him so.

Cinna
　O Caesar!
Caesar　　　　　Hence! Wilt thou lift up Olympus?
Decius
　Great Caesar!
Caesar　　　　　Doth not Brutus bootless kneel?   75
Casca
　Speak, hands, for me!

They stab CAESAR. CASCA *strikes the first*, BRUTUS
the last blow

Caesar
　Et tu, Brute?—Then fall, Caesar!

Dies

Cinna
　Liberty! Freedom! Tyranny is dead!
　Run hence, proclaim, cry it about the streets.
Cassius
　Some to the common pulpits, and cry out   80
　'Liberty, freedom, and enfranchisement!'
Brutus
　People and Senators, be not affrighted.
　Fly not; stand still. Ambition's debt is paid.

115

87. *quite confounded with this mutiny:* 'quite overcome by this revolution.'

88-9. Metellus fears a counter-attack by some of Caesar's friends. Brutus's interruption shows that he doesn't think anything like that is at all likely.

93-4. Publius was obviously an old man, of no importance in the play except to illustrate, even at this tense moment, Brutus's concern for others as well as his desire to restore order.
94. *do your age some mischief:* 'do some harm to a feeble old man like you.'
95-6. *and let . . . we the doers:* 'let nobody take the responsibility for what has been done except us, the ones who have done it.'

97. *amaz'd:* astounded, shocked.
97-8. Shakespeare has already conveyed the confusion that immediately follows the death of Caesar by means of the tense, jerky conversation and the general sense of alarm. Here, a much deeper sense of bewilderment is expressed. An assassination is always a terrible thing, but at a time when the ordinary people depended far more than they do today upon the personal authority of one ruler, it was much more terrifying.
100-1. *'tis but . . . stand upon:* 'it's the exact date (of death) and how long life will last that really worries men.'

102-6. It is impossible to take entirely seriously these suggestions by Brutus and Cassius that they have done Caesar a favour by killing him. But the tendency to joke in a nervous way is quite normal amongst people at times of stress and this is what Brutus and Cassius seem to be doing as a natural way of relieving the tension of the situation.

Casca
Go to the pulpit, Brutus.
Decius
And Cassius too.   85
Brutus
Where's Publius?
Cinna
Here, quite confounded with this mutiny.
Metellus
Stand fast together, lest some friend of Caesar's
Should chance—
Brutus
Talk not of standing. Publius, good cheer!   90
There is no harm intended to your person,
Nor to no Roman else. So tell them, Publius.
Cassius
And leave us, Publius, lest that the people,
Rushing on us, should do your age some mischief.
Brutus
Do so; and let no man abide this deed   95
But we the doers.

Re-enter TREBONIUS

Cassius
Where is Antony?
Trebonius   Fled to his house amaz'd.
Men, wives, and children, stare, cry out, and run,
As it were doomsday.
Brutus   Fates, we will know your
        pleasures.
That we shall die, we know; 'tis but the time,   100
And drawing days out, that men stand upon.
Cassius
Why, he that cuts off twenty years of life
Cuts off so many years of fearing death.
Brutus
Grant that, and then is death a benefit.

117

105. *abridg'd:* shortened.

106-11. This idea seems revolting and unnatural to us today and also surprising in that it is suggested by Brutus, supposedly the most reasonable and level-headed in the group. But it does show Brutus doing what he originally intended—making the murder of Caesar a kind of *ritual sacrifice* (Act II, Scene i, lines 165 & 173), and the bloody swords and arms of the assassins will be, to him, a symbol of the triumph of liberty as well as a means of letting the people know who had actually murdered Caesar. In addition, Calphurnia's dream is only too vividly fulfilled.

112-14. Cassius foresees the time when, in later ages and in different countries, the death of Caesar will be re-enacted on the stage.

114. 'In countries not yet in existence and in languages not yet created.'

115. *in sport:* i.e. as a show or spectacle.

116. *Pompey's basis:* at the foot of Pompey's statue.
along: stretched out.

118. *knot:* small group.

121. *grace his heels:* give honourable support by walking just behind him.

126. *prostrate:* kneeling (usually, lying down.)
127. *honest:* honourable.
127-8. Note each of the words used to describe Brutus and Caesar. They are all equally words of praise and do not show any preference for one or the other. Thus, they do not give any clear indication about Antony's intentions but since they appeal to Brutus's sense of honour, they are rightly judged by Antony to be most likely to secure his own safety.
128. *royal:* noble.
132. *resolv'd:* satisfied.

So are we Caesar's friends, that have abridg'd   *105*
His time of fearing death. Stoop, Romans, stoop,
And let us bathe our hands in Caesar's blood
Up to the elbows, and besmear our swords.
Then walk we forth, even to the market-place,
And waving our red weapons o'er our heads,   *110*
Let's all cry 'Peace, freedom, and liberty!'

Cassius

Stoop then, and wash. How many ages hence
Shall this our lofty scene be acted over
In states unborn and accents yet unknown!

Brutus

How many times shall Caesar bleed in sport,   *115*
That now on Pompey's basis lies along
No worthier than the dust!

Cassius   So oft as that shall be,
So often shall the knot of us be call'd
The men that gave their country liberty.

Decius

What, shall we forth?

Cassius   Ay, every man away.   *120*
Brutus shall lead, and we will grace his heels
With the most boldest and best hearts of Rome.

Enter a SERVANT

Brutus

Soft, who comes here? A friend of Antony's.

Servant

Thus, Brutus, did my master bid me kneel;
Thus did Mark Antony bid me fall down;   *125*
And, being prostrate, thus he bade me say:
Brutus is noble, wise, valiant, and honest;
Caesar was mighty, bold, royal, and loving.
Say I love Brutus, and I honour him;
Say I fear'd Caesar, honour'd him and lov'd him.   *130*
If Brutus will vouchsafe that Antony
May safely come to him, and be resolv'd

119

133. *How:* for what reason.

137-8. *Thorough the hazards:* . . . *true faith:* 'Through all the risks of this uncertain state of affairs, with complete loyalty.'

141. *so please him:* 'if it pleases him to.'

144. *well to friend:* as a firm friend.

145. *mind:* feeling, sense of foreboding.
146-7. *my misgiving:* . . . *to the purpose:* 'my doubts always turn out to be quite near the truth.'

149. Antony immediately addresses the body of Caesar and ignores the conspirators. Though Brutus has guaranteed his safety, Antony is clearly in some danger at this first meeting after the murder and by addressing the dead Caesar he makes it difficult for Brutus and Cassius to interfere without appearing to be very 'dishonourable'. Thus, he gets over the first few tricky moments but there is no reason to suppose that he is not perfectly sincere in the actual words he uses.
151. *this little measure:* 'this insignificant amount.'
153. The expressions here refer to the old practice of drawing off blood from a sick person's veins as a supposed way of curing him (known as 'blood-letting'). In this case, it would be because he is swollen with disease (*rank*). The line is a good example of irony (the use of words with a special and not immediately obvious meaning) since the murder had nothing to do with physical sickness at all; but it is a reminder of the way in which Caesar's rule was regarded by Brutus and Ligarius (Act II, Scene i, lines 327-8) and of the other occasions on which disease is mentioned in the play.

How Caesar hath deserv'd to lie in death,
Mark Antony shall not love Caesar dead
So well as Brutus living; but will follow   *135*
The fortunes and affairs of noble Brutus
Thorough the hazards of this untrod state
With all true faith. So says my master Antony.

Brutus

Thy master is a wise and valiant Roman;
I never thought him worse.   *140*
Tell him, so please him come unto this place,
He shall be satisfied and, by my honour,
Depart untouch'd.

Servant   I'll fetch him presently.

Exit

Brutus

I know that we shall have him well to friend.

Cassius

I wish we may. But yet have I a mind   *145*
That fears him much; and my misgiving still
Falls shrewdly to the purpose.

Re-enter ANTONY

Brutus

But here comes Antony. Welcome, Mark Antony.

Antony

O mighty Caesar! dost thou lie so low?
Are all thy conquests, glories, triumphs, spoils,   *150*
Shrunk to this little measure? Fare thee well.
I know not, gentlemen, what you intend,
Who else must be let blood, who else is rank.

154-60. Antony's dramatic invitation to the conspirators to kill him is clearly designed to make his death *less* likely. But, once again, we should not make the mistake of assuming that he is not sincere in his feelings for Caesar.

155-7. *nor no instrument . . . this world:* 'nor is there any weapon (to kill me) nearly as good as your own swords that have been enriched by being stained with the noblest blood of all.'

158. *bear me hard:* see Act II, Scene i, line 215.

159. *purpled:* stained with blood.

reek and smoke: the words meant much the same thing. Their hands are still steaming with the hot blood of Caesar.

160-1. *Live a thousand . . . to die:* 'If I live a thousand years, I shall never be quite so ready to die as I am now.'

162. *mean:* means, method.

163. *cut off:* killed.

171-3. *And pity . . . Caesar:* 'Just as one fire will drive out another, so our pity for Rome overcame our pity for Caesar and caused this deed to be done.'

174. *leaden points:* i.e. blunt points. A way of saying that they did not mean to harm Antony.

175-6. A confusing passage in which the difficult part to understand is the phrase *in strength of malice* because Brutus is offering friendship, not malice or hostility. The phrase might mean 'though apparently full of malice (because our arms are covered with blood), our hearts are full of brotherly affection towards you.'

178-9. 'You shall have as much influence as anybody in the new appointments that have to be made.' Brutus has just offered friendship; Cassius offers a share of the power that now has to be taken over by important men in Rome. In this way, an essential difference between the two men, one practical, even materialistic, the other idealistic, is revealed.

180. *appeas'd:* calmed, satisfied.

182. *deliver:* explain to.

184. *I doubt not of:* 'I have no doubts about'. We shall see shortly what Antony's true feelings are but, for the present, they have to be concealed in the presence of his enemies. However, from time to time, flashes of his hatred are revealed in suggestions and hints behind their more obvious and apparently harmless meanings. This line is an example of such irony.

If I myself, there is no hour so fit
As Caesar's death's hour; nor no instrument   *155*
Of half that worth as those your swords, made rich
With the most noble blood of all this world.
I do beseech ye, if you bear me hard,
Now, whilst your purpled hands do reek and smoke,
Fulfil your pleasure. Live a thousand years,   *160*
I shall not find myself so apt to die.
No place will please me so, no mean of death,
As here by Caesar, and by you cut off,
The choice and master spirits of this age.

Brutus

O Antony! beg not your death of us.   *165*
Though now we must appear bloody and cruel,
As by our hands and this our present act
You see we do; yet see you but our hands,
And this the bleeding business they have done.
Our hearts you see not; they are pitiful;   *170*
And pity to the general wrong of Rome,
As fire drives out fire, so pity pity,
Hath done this deed on Caesar. For your part,
To you our swords have leaden points, Mark
      Antony;
Our arms in strength of malice, and our hearts   *175*
Of brothers' temper, do receive you in
With all kind love, good thoughts, and reverence.

Cassius

Your voice shall be as strong as any man's
In the disposing of new dignities.

Brutus

Only be patient till we have appeas'd   *180*
The multitude, beside themselves with fear,
And then we will deliver you the cause
Why I, that did love Caesar when I struck him,
Have thus proceeded.

Antony   I doubt not of your wisdom.
Let each man render me his bloody hand.   *185*

189. *my valiant Casca:* an example of very strong and thinly concealed irony. Casca had stabbed Caesar from behind (see Act V, Scene i, lines 43-4).

192-4. Antony means that his reputation is in such a difficult position that, whatever attitude he takes, they will regard him as equally bad—a coward if he makes friends with them for the safety of his own skin, or a flatterer if he does so for any other reason, since he had always been a close friend of Caesar's.

197. *dearer:* more deeply.

200. *Most noble!* This might refer to Caesar. Antony would thus be breaking off his speech to address the dead Caesar in admiring terms. But it might refer to *foes* and then be another example of irony.

corse: corpse, body.

203-4. 'It would really be better for me (to weep floods of tears) than to form a friendly agreement with your enemies.'

205. *Julius:* an unusual way of addressing Caesar. This use of the fore-name shows Antony's strong friendship for Caesar and reveals that he has forgotten, for the moment, that he is in the presence of Caesar's murderers. Though he has been acting a part for most of the time since his entry and is determined (as we see shortly) to revenge the death of Caesar, at this point and at least as far as line 210 he seems to be speaking with completely sincere feeling.

bay'd: brought to bay, like a hunted deer, i.e. at the point when the deer cannot escape and has to stand and fight to the death.

207. The image, in which Caesar is seen as a hunted animal with the conspirators as hunters, is continued, and here the reference is to the custom of the hunters marking themselves with some of the blood of the dead animal (as is sometimes done today in England to young people on their first fox-hunt).

Lethe: strictly, the river in Hades, frequently mentioned in ancient Greek and Roman mythology. To drink from it led to forgetfulness of the past. Here, it seems to refer to Caesar's blood, the pouring out of which (like a river) led to his death. It is very difficult to paraphrase this line in a way that does justice to Antony's sense of horror. 'Horribly smeared with all the revolting evidence of your death', might come near it.

208-9. Antony sees Caesar as a hart (male deer) which roamed throughout the entire world (the Roman Empire) and also the 'heart' (notice the pun) *of* the world.

210. *strucken:* wounded, struck down.

212. Cassius thinks Antony has gone far enough and interrupts him.

214. *cold modesty:* very moderate praise.

216. *compact:* understanding, agreement.

217. *prick'd:* listed, counted.

First, Marcus Brutus, will I shake with you;
Next, Caius Cassius, do I take your hand;
Now, Decius Brutus, yours; now yours, Metellus;
Yours, Cinna; and, my valiant Casca, yours.
Though last, not least in love, yours, good
    Trebonius.   *190*
Gentlemen all—alas, what shall I say?
My credit now stands on such slippery ground
That one of two bad ways you must conceit me,
Either a coward or a flatterer.
That I did love thee, Caesar, O, 'tis true!   *195*
If then thy spirit look upon us now,
Shall it not grieve thee dearer than thy death
To see thy Antony making his peace,
Shaking the bloody fingers of thy foes,
Most noble! in the presence of thy corse?   *200*
Had I as many eyes as thou hast wounds,
Weeping as fast as they stream forth thy blood,
It would become me better than to close
In terms of friendship with thine enemies.
Pardon me, Julius! Here wast thou bay'd, brave
    hart;   *205*
Here didst thou fall; and here thy hunters stand,
Sign'd in thy spoil, and crimson'd in thy lethe.
O world, thou wast the forest to this hart;
And this indeed, O world, the heart of thee!
How like a deer strucken by many princes   *210*
Dost thou here lie!
Cassius
  Mark Antony—
Antony   Pardon me, Caius Cassius.
The enemies of Caesar shall say this;
Then, in a friend, it is cold modesty.
Cassius
  I blame you not for praising Caesar so;   *215*
But what compact mean you to have with us?
Will you be prick'd in number of our friends,

218. *on:* carry on, proceed.

219. *Therefore I took your hands:* 'I shook hands with you to indicate that I wanted to join you.'

222. *Upon this hope:* 'on condition that.'

224. 'If there were no such explanations, this would indeed be a dreadful sight.'
225. *good regard:* sound justifications.

228. *suitor:* see Act II, Scene iii, line 9.

229. 'Take his body to the market-place and display it there.'

231. 'Make a speech in the course of the funeral ceremony.' Of course this will give him the opportunity he wants and is therefore highly dangerous to the conspirators. Funeral orations were normally given by close friends and colleagues of the dead man.
233-6. Cassius, as always, understands the practical dangers much better than Brutus does.

239. *protest:* announce.

241-2. Brutus says that he will make it clear to the crowd that the conspirators are perfectly willing for the dead Caesar to have all the normal customs and ceremonies that such a great man would be entitled to at his funeral.
243-52. Brutus obviously makes a great mistake in allowing Antony to speak, as we see later. But his reasons for doing so seem quite sound at the time. Brutus is to speak first and puts some severe restrictions on what Antony can say. In particular, he argues that to have Caesar's best friend speaking almost as a member of the conspirators' party, is an immense advantage to them.

Or shall we on, and not depend on you?
Antony
  Therefore I took your hands; but was indeed
  Sway'd from the point by looking down on Caesar. *220*
  Friends am I with you all, and love you all,
  Upon this hope, that you shall give me reasons
  Why and wherein Caesar was dangerous.
Brutus
  Or else were this a savage spectacle.
  Our reasons are so full of good regard *225*
  That were you, Antony, the son of Caesar,
  You should be satisfied.
Antony   That's all I seek;
  And am moreover suitor that I may
  Produce his body to the market-place
  And, in the pulpit, as becomes a friend, *230*
  Speak in the order of his funeral.
Brutus
  You shall, Mark Antony.
Cassius   Brutus, a word with you.
  [*Aside to* BRUTUS] You know not what you do. Do
      not consent
  That Antony speak in his funeral.
  Know you how much the people may be mov'd *235*
  By that which he will utter?
Brutus [*Aside to* CASSIUS]   By your pardon—
  I will myself into the pulpit first,
  And show the reason of our Caesar's death.
  What Antony shall speak, I will protest
  He speaks by leave and by permission; *240*
  And that we are contented Caesar shall
  Have all true rites and lawful ceremonies.
  It shall advantage more than do us wrong.
Cassius
  I know not what may fall. I like it not.
Brutus
  Mark Antony, here, take you Caesar's body. *245*

258. *the tide of times:* the whole course of history.

260-1. Caesar's wounds are compared with mouths that 'cry out' for Antony to condemn the murder and predict terrible consequences.

265. *cumber:* burden, weigh down.

266. *in use:* common.

266-8. Antony foresees that there will be so much slaughter and horror in the land that mothers will look upon the deaths of their own children almost with pleasure.

269. *quartered:* chopped up into pieces.

270. 'Pity will cease to exist because dreadful things have become everyday events.'

271. *ranging:* roaming in search of victims.

272. *Até:* a goddess supposed to cause men to perform deeds of violence. Generally regarded as the goddess of Revenge.

274. *Havoc!* This was a military term, meaning that 'total war' was to be waged i.e. no mercy given, no prisoners taken. At about the time this play was written, only the king had the right to give this order. *dogs of war:* this suggests the unleashing of large dogs, such as mastiffs, to tear their victim to pieces. 'Famine, sword and fire' are compared with hounds in a warlike passage in *Henry V.*

You shall not in your funeral speech blame us,
But speak all good you can devise of Caesar;
And say you do't by our permission;
Else shall you not have any hand at all
About his funeral. And you shall speak   *250*
In the same pulpit whereto I am going,
After my speech is ended.

Antony   Be it so;
I do desire no more.

Brutus

Prepare the body then, and follow us.

                    Exeunt all but ANTONY

Antony

O, pardon me, thou bleeding piece of earth,   *255*
That I am meek and gentle with these butchers!
Thou art the ruins of the noblest man
That ever lived in the tide of times.
Woe to the hand that shed this costly blood!
Over thy wounds now do I prophesy—   *260*
Which like dumb mouths do ope their ruby lips
To beg the voice and utterance of my tongue—
A curse shall light upon the limbs of men;
Domestic fury and fierce civil strife
Shall cumber all the parts of Italy;   *265*
Blood and destruction shall be so in use,
And dreadful objects so familiar,
That mothers shall but smile when they behold
Their infants quartered with the hands of war,
All pity chok'd with custom of fell deeds;   *270*
And Caesar's spirit, ranging for revenge,
With Até by his side come hot from hell,
Shall in these confines with a monarch's voice
Cry 'Havoc!' and let slip the dogs of war,

275-6. 'Consequently, this foul deed will smell to heaven with the stink of corpses, crying out to be buried.' This speech is one of the most powerful and bitter in the play. Now that he is alone, Antony expresses his true feelings without restraint and the constant repetition of ideas concerned with destruction, slaughter and their consequences is not just a prediction of future events but an indication of the strength of Antony's feelings. As Shakespeare has so far swayed our feelings to some extent in favour of Brutus, the speech also serves to remind us that, after all, a terrible deed has been done.

284. *Passion:* sorrow.
285. *beads of sorrow:* tears.

288. 'Hurry back and tell him what has happened.'

291. *Hie:* hasten.

293-5. *There shall I . . . bloody men:* 'In the market-place I will test in my speech how the people have reacted to the result of the cruelty of these bloodthirsty men.'

296. *discourse:* explain.

That this foul deed shall smell above the earth   *275*
With carrion men, groaning for burial.

Enter Octavius' SERVANT

You serve Octavius Caesar, do you not?
Servant
I do, Mark Antony.
Antony
Caesar did write for him to come to Rome.
Servant
He did receive his letters, and is coming,   *280*
And bid me say to you by word of mouth—

Seeing the body

O Caesar!
Antony
Thy heart is big, get thee apart and weep.
Passion, I see, is catching; for mine eyes,
Seeing those beads of sorrow stand in thine,   *285*
Began to water. Is thy master coming?
Servant
He lies to-night within seven leagues of Rome.
Antony
Post back with speed, and tell him what hath
    chanc'd.
Here is a mourning Rome, a dangerous Rome,
No Rome of safety for Octavius yet;   *290*
Hie hence and tell him so. Yet stay awhile;
Thou shalt not back till I have borne this corse
Into the market-place. There shall I try,
In my oration, how the people take
The cruel issue of these bloody men;   *295*
According to the which thou shalt discourse
To young Octavius of the state of things.
Lend me your hand.

Exeunt with CAESAR'S body

JULIUS CAESAR

SCENE II

Now follows one of the finest scenes in the play and perhaps the best of its kind ever written. Brutus, the honourable and widely-respected leader of the murderers, tries to explain why Caesar had to be killed and in a carefully prepared and convincing speech he does succeed in persuading the crowd that justice has been done. But Brutus has not properly reckoned with Antony who, in a remarkable piece of mob oratory, turns the tables completely and by the end of the scene has destroyed all hopes the conspirators ever had of establishing themselves in Rome and applying the 'redress' that Brutus longed for. Comparisons between these two speeches are inevitably made and it is often assumed that Antony's is the better if only because it is completely successful in wiping out the whole effect of what Brutus has said. This should not blind us to the sincerity and skill of the first oration which would certainly have received applause (as a speech) in the Roman Senate or the English House of Lords. But its very quality and strength is also its weakness, for Brutus is perfectly fair and honest and reasonable whereas Antony is hypocritical, dishonest and highly emotional, and he has to be if he is to win over the people. And yet Antony has one vital aspect of the truth that outweighs everything else—the mangled body of a once great man.

Both speakers are trying to establish their own power by appealing to the plebeians whose support they depend upon completely. What kind of people these plebeians are, in Shakespeare's eyes, is painfully obvious in this scene.

Stage Direction. *Plebeians:* the common people or Roman mob.

1. *satisfied.* They demand an explanation for Caesar's death.

2. *give me audience:* grant me a hearing.

4. *part:* split up.

10. *severally:* separately.

14-16. *Believe me . . . believe:* 'Believe me, because I am an honourable man, and remember my honourable reputation so that you may be more ready to believe me.' The style is very formal, the first three sentences being based on a pattern in which each sentence ends almost exactly as it begins.

16-17. *Censure me . . . judge:* 'Judge me according to your reason, and use your powers of reason to the full in order to judge me more accurately.' So far, Brutus's words have sounded very impressive but have not meant very much. In contrast with Antony's speech, which occurs later, Brutus speaks in prose. In Shakespeare, prose usually goes with situations and speeches that do not express very strong feeling and here it is suitable because Brutus is basing his argument on reason rather than emotion.

20-4. These lines show a pattern of contrasts, 'less . . . more'; 'living . . . die', etc.

SCENE II—*Rome. The Forum*

   Enter BRUTUS *and* CASSIUS, *with the* PLEBEIANS

Citizens
  We will be satisfied! Let us be satisfied!
Brutus
  Then follow me, and give me audience, friends.
  Cassius, go you into the other street,
  And part the numbers.
  Those that will hear me speak, let 'em stay here;   *5*
  Those that will follow Cassius, go with him;
  And public reasons shall be rendered
  Of Caesar's death.
First Plebeian   I will hear Brutus speak.
Second Plebeian
  I will hear Cassius, and compare their reasons,
  When severally we hear them rendered.   *10*

   Exit CASSIUS, *with some of the* PLEBEIANS. BRUTUS
         goes into the pulpit

Third Plebeian
  The noble Brutus is ascended. Silence!
Brutus
  Be patient till the last.
  Romans, countrymen, and lovers! hear me for my
  cause, and be silent, that you may hear. Believe me
  for mine honour, and have respect to mine honour, *15*
  that you may believe. Censure me in your wisdom,
  and awake your senses, that you may the better judge.
  If there be any in this assembly, any dear friend of
  Caesar's, to him I say that Brutus' love to Caesar was
  no less than his. If then that friend demand why *20*
  Brutus rose against Caesar, this is my answer: Not
  that I lov'd Caesar less, but that I lov'd Rome more.

25-6. *As Caesar lov'd . . . honour him.* Here, words are linked with one another in pairs, 'lov'd . . . weep', 'fortunate . . . rejoice', leading to the climax 'ambition . . . slew'.

27-9. *There is tears . . . ambition.* A similar construction.

29-31. *Who is here . . . have I offended.* The repeated phrase again emphasizes the rigid formality of Brutus's speech which is logically sound but shows little human feeling. It is almost as though Brutus is trying to justify Caesar's death on mathematical grounds!

38-9. *The question . . . in the Capitol:* 'The whole matter of his death has been written down and the record is in the Capitol.' Of course, there wouldn't have been time for this to be done, but in the theatre small mistakes of this kind are not important.
39-41. *his glory . . . death:* 'the glory which is due to him not being minimised nor the faults which caused his death exaggerated.'

44. *a place in the commonwealth:* a position of importance in Rome.

45-8. Just as Antony practically invited the conspirators to kill him after Caesar's death, so Brutus makes a similar offer to the crowd, confident that they do not want him to die and that they will support him all the more for his apparent willingness to sacrifice himself.

49-54. The crowd go wild with enthusiasm for Brutus, the third citizen even suggesting that he should be given the very title that provoked the conspiracy.

Had you rather Caesar were living, and die all slaves,
than that Caesar were dead, to live all free men?
As Caesar lov'd me, I weep for him; as he was   *25*
fortunate, I rejoice at it; as he was valiant, I honour
him; but—as he was ambitious, I slew him. There is
tears for his love; joy for his fortune; honour for his
valour; and death for his ambition. Who is here so
base that would be a bondman? If any, speak; for   *30*
him have I offended. Who is here so rude that would
not be a Roman? If any, speak; for him have I
offended. Who is here so vile that will not love his
country? If any, speak; for him have I offended. I
pause for a reply.   *35*

All

None, Brutus, none.

Brutus

Then none have I offended. I have done no more
to Caesar than you shall do to Brutus. The question
of his death is enroll'd in the Capitol; his glory not
extenuated, wherein he was worthy; nor his offences   *40*
enforc'd, for which he suffered death.

   Enter MARK ANTONY *and* OTHERS *with Caesar's body*
Here comes his body, mourn'd by Mark Antony,
who, though he had no hand in his death, shall
receive the benefit of his dying, a place in the commonwealth, as which of you shall not? With this   *45*
I depart, that, as I slew my best lover for the good
of Rome, I have the same dagger for myself, when it
shall please my country to need my death.

All

Live, Brutus! live, live!

First Plebeian

Bring him with triumph home unto his house.   *50*

Second Plebeian

Give him a statue with his ancestors.

Third Plebeian

Let him be Caesar.

52-3. *Caesar's better parts . . . Brutus:* 'Brutus will be a better Caesar than Caesar himself.'

59-60. *Do grace . . . glories:* 'Show respect for Caesar's body and for Antony's speech which is in praise of Caesar.'

65. *chair:* pulpit.

67. *beholding:* obliged, indebted.

68-70. Shakespeare emphasizes how strongly the plebeians are in favour of Brutus when Antony begins to speak.

Fourth Plebeian   Caesar's better parts
  Shall be crown'd in Brutus.
First Plebeian
  We'll bring him to his house with shouts and
      clamours.
Brutus
  My countrymen—
Second Plebeian   Peace, silence! Brutus speaks.   55
First Plebeian
  Peace, ho!
Brutus
  Good countrymen, let me depart alone,
  And for my sake stay here with Antony.
  Do grace to Caesar's corpse, and grace his speech
  Tending to Caesar's glories, which Mark Antony   60
  By our permission, is allow'd to make.
  I do entreat you, not a man depart
  Save I alone, till Antony have spoke.

                Exit

First Plebeian
  Stay, ho! and let us hear Mark Antony.
Third Plebeian
  Let him go up into the public chair.   65
  We'll hear him. Noble Antony, go up.
Antony
  For Brutus' sake I am beholding to you.

                Goes up

Fourth Plebeian
  What does he say of Brutus?
Third Plebeian   He says, for Brutus'
      sake
  He finds himself beholding to us all.
Fourth Plebeian
  'Twere best he speak no harm of Brutus here.   70
First Plebeian
  This Caesar was a tyrant.

137

76-9. Antony, knowing the mood of the crowd (note when he entered and what he would have heard), declares that he has no intention of praising Caesar. He adds that, when people die, their evil deeds tend to be remembered while their virtues are forgotten. It is doubtful whether this is really true but it serves the purpose of suggesting, indirectly, that Caesar did have some good in him.

81. *If:* This word provides a very faint hint that Caesar might not have been ambitious after all. But Antony dare not speak freely yet.
82. *answer'd it:* paid for or suffered for it.

91. *general coffers:* the treasury of Rome.

92. 'Was this an example of Caesar's ambition?'

93. Antony is describing Caesar as, above all, a man with warm human sympathy for others; a faithful friend (line 87) and one who wept at the sufferings of the poor.
94. 'A really ambitious man should be much harder and more ruthless.'

97. *on the:* at the feast of.

101. At about this point, Antony begins to use the word *honourable* with at least a hint of irony, but hurriedly appears to correct any impression that he is opposing Brutus in case he has gone too far.

Third Plebeian   Nay, that's certain.
  We are blest that Rome is rid of him.
Second Plebeian
  Peace! let us hear what Antony can say.
Antony
  You gentle Romans—
All   Peace, ho! let us hear him.
Antony
  Friends, Romans, countrymen, lend me your ears;   75
  I come to bury Caesar, not to praise him.
  The evil that men do lives after them;
  The good is oft interred with their bones;
  So let it be with Caesar. The noble Brutus
  Hath told you Caesar was ambitious.   80
  If it were so, it was a grievous fault;
  And grievously hath Caesar answer'd it.
  Here, under leave of Brutus and the rest—
  For Brutus is an honourable man;
  So are they all, all honourable men—   85
  Come I to speak in Caesar's funeral.
  He was my friend, faithful and just to me;
  But Brutus says he was ambitious,
  And Brutus is an honourable man.
  He hath brought many captives home to Rome,   90
  Whose ransoms did the general coffers fill;
  Did this in Caesar seem ambitious?
  When that the poor have cried, Caesar hath wept;
  Ambition should be made of sterner stuff.
  Yet Brutus says he was ambitious;   95
  And Brutus is an honourable man.
  You all did see that on the Lupercal
  I thrice presented him a kingly crown,
  Which he did thrice refuse. Was this ambition?
  Yet Brutus says he was ambitious;   100
  And sure he is an honourable man.
  I speak not to disprove what Brutus spoke,

139

103. The things that Antony 'knows' include some things that the people can see for themselves as well, for example, the filling of the treasury with ransom money and the fact that Caesar refused the crown three times. Brutus, in his speech, gave no facts at all but relied on a general accusation of Caesar's ambition.

106-9. Antony concludes the first part of his speech with an impressive display of emotion—indignation that the plebeians will not even express their sorrow at Caesar's death, and personal grief. A good deal of this is obviously false and hypocritical but it is already clear that Antony has a much better grip on the crowd than Brutus has. His language is simpler, clearer and more direct and the rhythm of the blank verse makes his ideas come across with much greater force.

112-13. *Has he, masters! . . . in his place:* 'He certainly has, my friends, and the change will not be for the better.' Note that it was the third citizen who wanted Brutus to be Caesar!

116. *some will dear abide it:* 'somebody will pay dearly for this.'

120. *But:* only.

122. 'The lowest person is now too high to pay respect to him.'

123-7. Antony claims to want to avoid 'mutiny and rage' but in saying so he drops the idea into the people's minds and thereby helps to create the situation he wants.

124. *mutiny:* uprising, riot.

128. Antony groups Caesar, himself and the crowd together in opposition to the *honourable men.*

But here I am to speak what I do know.
You all did love him once, not without cause;
What cause witholds you, then, to mourn for him?   *105*
O judgment, thou art fled to brutish beasts,
And men have lost their reason! Bear with me;
My heart is in the coffin there with Caesar,
And I must pause till it come back to me.

First Plebeian
  Methinks there is much reason in his sayings.   *110*
Second Plebeian
  If thou consider rightly of the matter,
  Caesar has had great wrong.
Third Plebeian   Has he, masters!
  I fear there will a worse come in his place.
Fourth Plebeian
  Mark'd ye his words? He would not take the crown;
  Therefore 'tis certain he was not ambitious.   *115*
First Plebeian
  If it be found so, some will dear abide it.
Second Plebeian
  Poor soul! his eyes are red as fire with weeping.
Third Plebeian
  There's not a nobler man in Rome than Antony.
Fourth Plebeian
  Now mark him, he begins again to speak.
Antony
  But yesterday the word of Caesar might   *120*
  Have stood against the world: now lies he there,
  And none so poor to do him reverence.
  O masters, if I were dispos'd to stir
  Your hearts and minds to mutiny and rage,
  I should do Brutus wrong, and Cassius wrong,   *125*
  Who, you all know, are honourable men.
  I will not do them wrong; I rather choose
  To wrong the dead, to wrong myself and you,
  Than I will wrong such honourable men.
  But here's a parchment with the seal of Caesar   *130*

131-3. Antony knows perfectly well that showing the will and hinting at its contents is the best way of persuading the mob to insist that he should read it.

135. *napkins.* These would be dipped in the blood and kept as relics. See Act II, Scene ii, lines 88-9.

138-9. *Bequeathing . . . issue:* 'Passing it on to their children as a valuable inheritance.'

143. *meet:* right, proper.

144. Compare these words with those of Marullus in Act I, Scene i, line 36.

147. In one sentence Antony tells them something—and that they mustn't know it!

152. *o'ershot myself:* gone too far.

153-4. By now, the word *honourable* is used wholly sarcastically and this is emphasized by the harsh words, suggestive of violence, that follow.

I found it in his closet—'tis his will.
Let but the commons hear this testament,
Which, pardon me, I do not mean to read,
And they would go and kiss dead Caesar's wounds
And dip their napkins in his sacred blood;   *135*
Yea, beg a hair of him for memory
And, dying, mention it within their wills,
Bequeathing it as a rich legacy
Unto their issue.

Fourth Plebeian

We'll hear the will. Read it, Mark Antony.   *140*

All

The will, the will! We will hear Caesar's will.

Antony

Have patience, gentle friends, I must not read it;
It is not meet you know how Caesar lov'd you.
You are not wood, you are not stones, but men;
And being men, hearing the will of Caesar,   *145*
It will inflame you, it will make you mad.
'Tis good you know not that you are his heirs;
For if you should, O, what would come of it?

Fourth Plebeian

Read the will; we'll hear it, Antony!
You shall read us the will—Caesar's will.   *150*

Antony

Will you be patient? Will you stay awhile?
I have o'ershot myself to tell you of it.
I fear I wrong the honourable men
Whose daggers have stabb'd Caesar; I do fear it.

Fourth Plebeian

They were traitors. Honourable men!   *155*

All

The will! the testament!

Second Plebeian

They were villains, murderers. The will! Read the
will.

159. He pretends that he has no alternative but to read the will.

162. *descend*. Antony was probably intended to give his speech, up to this point, from the balcony of the Elizabethan stage. Now, he would come down on to the main stage and the mob would have to clear part of it for him so that Antony, and Caesar's body, could be seen by the audience.

171. Antony now knows exactly how to handle his audience and introduces a quiet and sentimental note after the hysteria over the will. The reference to the familiar mantle and the summer's evening creates a nostalgic atmosphere that is shattered by the detailed examples of the stab wounds. It is, of course, unlikely that Antony would know exactly who stabbed where, but in the circumstances this hardly matters.

175. *Nervii:* a tribe over which Caesar gained one of his finest victories.

177. *envious:* malicious.

178. *well-beloved.* Antony says this with biting sarcasm.

179. *steel:* sword.

181-2. The strange idea here is that Caesar's blood gushed out in a flood from Brutus's stab wound, like somebody rushing to the door of a house to answer a knock.

183. *angel:* favourite; dearest friend.

Antony

    You will compel me, then, to read the will?

    Then make a ring about the corpse of Caesar,   *160*

    And let me show you him that made the will.

    Shall I descend? and will you give me leave?

All

    Come down.

Second Plebeian

    Descend.

ANTONY comes down

Third Plebeian

    You shall have leave.   *165*

Fourth Plebeian

    A ring! Stand round.

First Plebeian

    Stand from the hearse, stand from the body.

Second Plebeian

    Room for Antony, most noble Antony!

Antony

    Nay, press not so upon me; stand far off.

All

    Stand back. Room! Bear back.   *170*

Antony

    If you have tears, prepare to shed them now.

    You all do know this mantle. I remember

    The first time ever Caesar put it on;

    'Twas on a summer's evening, in his tent,

    That day he overcame the Nervii.   *175*

    Look! in this place ran Cassius' dagger through;

    See what a rent the envious Casca made;

    Through this the well-beloved Brutus stabb'd,

    And as he pluck'd his cursed steel away,

    Mark how the blood of Caesar follow'd it,   *180*

    As rushing out of doors, to be resolv'd

    If Brutus so unkindly knock'd or no;

    For Brutus, as you know, was Caesar's angel.

185. *most unkindest:* 'most cruel' and 'most unnatural'. The double superlative emphasizes the meaning and was not regarded as bad English when the play was written.

187-8. *Ingratitude . . . vanquish'd him.* The idea is that Caesar was overcome by Brutus's ingratitude, in effect, rather than by any wounds. Though this cannot be taken literally, Caesar's '*Et tu, Brute?—Then fall, Caesar!*' gives some justification for what Antony says.

189-90. Pompey's statue running with blood might be intended as a sign of sympathy from one murdered man (Pompey) to another. More simply, and more likely, this part could refer to the splashing of Caesar's blood on to the statue.

192. Antony sees the 'fall' of Caesar as a blow to *all* the people of Rome.

195-6. *I perceive . . . drops:* 'I see you are affected by pity; your tears show your respect (for Caesar).'

197-8. *what weep . . . wounded?* 'Do you shed tears when all you see is Caesar's tattered clothing?'

199. Antony then whips away Caesar's mantle, exposing the mutilated body. This is planned by Antony to rouse the most violent emotion amongst the plebeians.

Judge, O you gods, how dearly Caesar lov'd him!
This was the most unkindest cut of all;   *185*
For when the noble Caesar saw him stab,
Ingratitude, more strong than traitors' arms,
Quite vanquish'd him. Then burst his mighty heart;
And in his mantle muffling up his face,
Even at the base of Pompey's statua,   *190*
Which all the while ran blood, great Caesar fell.
O, what a fall was there, my countrymen!
Then I, and you, and all of us fell down,
Whilst bloody treason flourish'd over us.
O, now you weep, and I perceive you feel   *195*
The dint of pity. These are gracious drops.
Kind souls, what weep you when you but behold
Our Caesar's vesture wounded? Look you here,
Here is himself, marr'd as you see with traitors.

First Plebeian
  O piteous spectacle!   *200*
Second Plebeian
  O noble Caesar!
Third Plebeian
  O woeful day!
Fourth Plebeian
  O traitors, villains!
First Plebeian
  O most bloody sight!
Second Plebeian
  We will be reveng'd.   *205*
All
  Revenge! About! Seek! Burn! Fire! Kill! Slay! Let
  not a traitor live!
Antony
  Stay, countrymen.
First Plebeian
  Peace there! Hear the noble Antony.
Second Plebeian
  We'll hear him, we'll follow him, we'll die with him. *210*

211-12. Again, Antony hypocritically pretends that he doesn't want to cause a riot.

216. These reasons, of course, were given first by Brutus but have been forgotten already.

218-19. As we can easily see, Antony is a much better orator than Brutus is, at least for this crowd and this occasion. An appearance of humility and a claim to be no more than an ordinary man are almost certain to win popularity with the plebeians, and Antony knows it.
221. *public leave to speak:* permission to speak in public.

222-4. *I have neither . . . men's blood:* 'I haven't the intelligence, verbal skill, character, bearing, power of expression or ability to project myself in a way to rouse men's passions.' Antony is just saying that he hasn't any of the qualities of a good orator, but of course he is lying; he knows he has.

229. *ruffle up:* rouse.
229-30. As in line 226, the idea is that Caesar's wounds are like mouths that can 'speak' much more effectively than Antony can.
231-2. Again, mutiny is mentioned, with exactly the desired effect.

Antony

Good friends, sweet friends, let me not stir you up
To such a sudden flood of mutiny.
They that have done this deed are honourable.
What private griefs they have, alas, I know not,
That made them do it; they are wise and
    honourable,   215
And will, no doubt, with reasons answer you.
I come not, friends, to steal away your hearts;
I am no orator, as Brutus is,
But, as you know me all, a plain blunt man,
That love my friend; and that they know full well   220
That gave me public leave to speak of him.
For I have neither wit, nor words, nor worth,
Action, nor utterance, nor the power of speech,
To stir men's blood; I only speak right on.
I tell you that which you yourselves do know;   225
Show you sweet Caesar's wounds, poor poor dumb
    mouths,
And bid them speak for me. But were I Brutus,
And Brutus Antony, there were an Antony
Would ruffle up your spirits, and put a tongue
In every wound of Caesar, that should move   230
The stones of Rome to rise and mutiny.

All

We'll mutiny.

First Plebeian

We'll burn the house of Brutus.

Third Plebeian

Away, then! Come seek the conspirators.

Antony

Yet hear me, countrymen; yet hear me speak.   235

All

Peace, ho! Hear Antony, most noble Antony.

Antony

Why, friends, you go to do you know not what.
Wherein hath Caesar thus deserv'd your loves?

240. So hysterical has the crowd become that they forget the will they demanded earlier and have to be reminded of it.

244. *seventy-five drachmas.* Dover Wilson says that this was worth 'about £3', i.e. a drachma was roughly equal to 4-5p. The important thing is that the sum Caesar leaves to the citizens is enough to excite the poorer ones, at least temporarily.
orchards: see Stage Direction Act II, Scene i.

250. *private arbours:* personal grounds or gardens.

252. *common pleasures:* recreation fields for public use.
253. *recreate:* exercise.

260. *pluck down:* take away by force.

261. *windows.* The plebeians intend to use anything that will burn for Caesar's funeral pyre. The word *windows* means wooden shutters.

Alas, you know not! I must tell you, then:
You have forgot the will I told you of.   240

All

Most true. The will! Let's stay and hear the will.

Antony

Here is the will, and under Caesar's seal:
To every Roman citizen he gives,
To every several man, seventy-five drachmas.

Second Plebeian

Most noble Caesar! We'll revenge his death.   245

Third Plebeian

O royal Caesar!

Antony

Hear me with patience.

All

Peace, ho!

Antony

Moreover, he hath left you all his walks,
His private arbours, and new-planted orchards,   250
On this side Tiber; he hath left them you,
And to your heirs for ever—common pleasures,
To walk abroad and recreate yourselves.
Here was a Caesar! When comes such another?

First Plebeian

Never, never! Come away, away!   255
We'll burn his body in the holy place,
And with the brands fire the traitors' houses.
Take up the body.

Second Plebeian

Go, fetch fire.

Third Plebeian

Pluck down benches.   260

Fourth Plebeian

Pluck down forms, windows, any thing.

Exeunt PLEBEIANS *with the body*

262-3. Antony's sincerity and love for Caesar have been pointed out in these notes. But he is cruel and cynical as well, and these lines reveal this fact very clearly.

264. Octavius's coming to Rome is in spite of Antony's warning in Act III, Scene i, lines 289-91.

266. *Lepidus.* He was the third most powerful man in Rome after the death of Caesar. Antony, Octavius and Lepidus formed a joint government between them, known as the 'Triumvirate' (rule by three men).

268. *upon a wish:* 'just when I want him.'
268-9. After his very successful speech, Antony is in a good mood and chuckles with pleasure.

271. *rid like madmen:* ridden away in panic. Just in time, no doubt, as the plebeians were after their blood!

SCENE III

Violence now turns into terrorism and Antony's 'mischief' strikes down the innocent as well as the guilty. In some ways, the wretched Cinna of this scene is like many other characters in the play. He feels an uncontrollable urge to wander out and put himself in great danger, though warned by an omen. In exactly the same way, the tribunes, Brutus, the other conspirators and, above all, Caesar himself, all defy either omens, warnings or plain common sense and step out on a path that leads to self-destruction.

1. *to-night:* again, the word means 'last night'.
2. 'These things have depressed my spirits.' The dream of feasting with Caesar was apparently a pleasant one, but on awaking he realizes that Caesar is dead.

Antony

Now let it work. Mischief, thou art afoot,
Take thou what course thou wilt.

Enter a SERVANT

How now, fellow!

Servant

Sir, Octavius is already come to Rome.

Antony

Where is he?   *265*

Servant

He and Lepidus are at Caesar's house.

Antony

And thither will I straight to visit him.
He comes upon a wish. Fortune is merry,
And in this mood will give us any thing.

Servant

I heard him say Brutus and Cassius   *270*
Are rid like madmen through the gates of Rome.

Antony

Belike they had some notice of the people,
How I had mov'd them. Bring me to Octavius.

Exeunt

SCENE III—*Rome. A street*

Enter CINNA *the* POET, *and after him the* PLEBEIANS

Cinna

I dreamt to-night that I did feast with Caesar,
And things unluckily charge my fantasy.
I have no will to wander forth of doors,
Yet something leads me forth.

5-12. These rapid questions, each one leaving no time for an answer, indicate the restless and dangerous mood of the plebeians.

18. *You'll bear me a bang for that:* 'I'll get you for that.'

First Plebeian
  What is your name?   5
Second Plebeian
  Whither are you going?
Third Plebeian
  Where do you dwell?
Fourth Plebeian
  Are you a married man or a bachelor?
Second Plebeian
  Answer every man directly.
First Plebeian
  Ay, and briefly.   10
Fourth Plebeian
  Ay, and wisely.
Third Plebeian
  Ay, and truly, you were best.
Cinna
  What is my name? Whither am I going? Where do I
  dwell? Am I a married man or a bachelor? Then to
  answer every man directly and briefly, wisely and   15
  truly: wisely, I say I am a bachelor.
Second Plebeian
  That's as much as to say they are fools that
  marry. You'll bear me a bang for that, I fear.
  Proceed directly.
Cinna
  Directly, I am going to Caesar's funeral.   20
First Plebeian
  As a friend or an enemy?
Cinna
  As a friend.
Second Plebeian
  That matter is answered directly.
Fourth Plebeian
  For your dwelling—briefly.
Cinna
  Briefly, I dwell by the Capitol.   25

29-32. The plebeians confuse this innocent poet for Cinna who was one of the conspirators but, such is their violent mood, they think up any excuse for killing him.

33-4. *pluck but . . . turn him going:* 'Just tear his heart out and shove him away.'

Third Plebeian

Your name, sir, truly.

Cinna

Truly, my name is Cinna.

First Plebeian

Tear him to pieces; he's a conspirator!

Cinna

I am Cinna the poet, I am Cinna the poet.

Fourth Plebeian

Tear him for his bad verses, tear him for his bad   *30*
verses!

Cinna

I am not Cinna the conspirator.

Fourth Plebeian

It is no matter, his name's Cinna; pluck but his
name out of his heart, and turn him going.

Third Plebeian

Tear him, tear him! Come, brands, ho! fire-brands!   *35*
To Brutus', to Cassius'! Burn all! Some to Decius'
house, and some to Casca's; some to Ligarius'. Away,
go!

Exeunt all the PLEBEIANS *with* CINNA

Whatever life in Rome was like under Caesar and whatever it might have been like under Brutus, the rule of the Triumvirate proves to be quite ruthless, with wholesale executions, even of their own flesh and blood. The cold-blooded way in which these men decide the deaths of their relatives tells us at once that Shakespeare does not want his audience's sympathy to lean towards Antony. The discussion about Lepidus serves to emphasize that, to Antony at least, power is the only thing that matters for the moment.

1. *prick'd:* marked on the list, we might say 'ticked'.

4-5. *Publius.* Not the Publius referred to by Brutus immediately after the murder of Caesar.

6. *with a spot I damn him.* Antony marks down his nephew for death with a mark on the list of names in front of him. 'I kill him with a dot.'

9. *cut off some charge in legacies:* 'cut down some of the expenses.' This would probably mean reducing the amount left to each citizen by Caesar's will and shows the dishonesty of the Triumvirs, and particularly Antony, who read out the will to the plebeians.

11. *Or . . . or:* 'either . . . or.'

12-13. *This . . . errands:* 'This Lepidus is a feeble, worthless individual, only fit to run errands for us.'

14. *threefold world.* The Triumvirs split up the Roman Empire into three parts and each took a share.

ACT FOUR

Enter ANTONY, OCTAVIUS, *and* LEPIDUS

Antony
  These many, then, shall die; their names are
      prick'd.
Octavius
  Your brother too must die. Consent you, Lepidus?
Lepidus
  I do consent.
Octavius   Prick him down, Antony.
Lepidus
  Upon condition Publius shall not live,
  Who is your sister's son, Mark Antony.   5
Antony
  He shall not live; look, with a spot I damn him.
  But, Lepidus, go you to Caesar's house;
  Fetch the will hither, and we shall determine
  How to cut off some charge in legacies.
Lepidus
  What, shall I find you here?   10
Octavius
  Or here or at the Capitol.

Exit LEPIDUS

Antony
  This is a slight unmeritable man,
  Meet to be sent on errands. Is it fit,
  The threefold world divided, he should stand
  One of the three to share it?

15-17. *So you . . . sentence:* 'You thought he was good enough and accepted his opinion about who should be executed under our death sentence.'

17. *proscription:* an order condemning people to death.

20. 'In order to shift some of the many slanderous accusations made against us on to him.' Lepidus is to be used as a scapegoat.

22. *business:* hard work.

25-6. *Then take . . . ass:* 'Then we unload the gold and turn him out to grass, like a useless old ass.' An ass is a rather despised beast of burden.

27. *graze in commons:* graze on the common land.

30. *appoint . . . provender:* give him a supply of fodder.

32. *wind:* turn.

33. *corporal:* physical.

34. *in some taste:* to a certain extent.
Antony seems to like manipulating people. He certainly did this with the plebeians and, as far as Lepidus is concerned, he can only think of him as an ass or horse—creatures used by men for their own purposes.

36. *barren-spirited:* unimaginative.

37. *abjects, orts:* bits thrown away and scraps left on a plate. He is contemptuously stressing Lepidus's lack of originality.

38-9. *Which . . . fashion.* He is interested only in things which are cast aside or soiled through much use by other men.

40. *a property:* a tool; a means to our own ends.

44. *means stretch'd:* our resources made to go as far as they can.

46-7. 'How under-cover dangers can best be brought to light and obvious threats best dealt with.'

160

Octavius   So you thought him,   15
  And took his voice who should be prick'd to die
  In our black sentence and proscription.
Antony
  Octavius, I have seen more days than you;
  And though we lay these honours on this man,
  To ease ourselves of divers sland'rous loads,   20
  He shall but bear them as the ass bears gold,
  To groan and sweat under the business,
  Either led or driven as we point the way;
  And having brought our treasure where we will,
  Then take we down his load, and turn him off,   25
  Like to the empty ass, to shake his ears
  And graze in commons.
Octavius   You may do your will;
  But he's a tried and valiant soldier.
Antony
  So is my horse, Octavius, and for that
  I do appoint him store of provender.   30
  It is a creature that I teach to fight,
  To wind, to stop, to run directly on,
  His corporal motion govern'd by my spirit.
  And, in some taste, is Lepidus but so:
  He must be taught, and train'd, and bid go forth   35
  A barren-spirited fellow; one that feeds
  On abjects, orts, and imitations,
  Which, out of use and stal'd by other men,
  Begin his fashion. Do not talk of him
  But as a property. And now, Octavius,   40
  Listen great things: Brutus and Cassius
  Are levying powers; we must straight make head;
  Therefore let our alliance be combin'd,
  Our best friends made, our means stretch'd;
  And let us presently go sit in council   45
  How covert matters may be best disclos'd,
  And open perils surest answered.

48-9. This figure of speech is from bear-baiting, a popular sport in Elizabethan England in which a bear was tied to a stake and then attacked by dogs. Octavius sees the Triumvirs as in the position of the bear, harassed and unable to move far. This is a reminder that, though the conspirators have been driven out of Rome, the Triumvirs' position is still insecure.

SCENE II

After being driven out of Rome, Brutus and Cassius make their way to Sardis, raising an army in the hope that they can eventually defeat the new regime in Rome. But they could never agree even on the details of the conspiracy itself and now, under the stress of events, the real differences between them are revealed in a violent quarrel. The reasons for this go deeper than the petty incidents that start it and are really rooted in the attitudes to life of the two men. Brutus's high moral principles sometimes seem to remove him from the world of ordinary men and women; Cassius's more down-to-earth nature, on the other hand, sometimes keeps him in touch with human beings. Certainly, the quarrel shows a harder and more intolerant Brutus than we have seen so far and a Cassius who is more human and emotionally strongly attached to his leader and friend. Their reconciliation is moving, but the news of Portia's death, Brutus's continued stubbornness in opposition to Cassius's practical advice and, most of all, the appearance of Caesar's ghost, all leave the atmosphere heavy with foreboding against the conspirators.

Though Scenes ii and iii are printed separately, Scene iii follows almost without a break and on the Elizabethan stage would take place on the inner stage, representing Brutus's tent, the troops moving off on either side at the end of Scene ii.

5. *do you salutation:* greet you.

6-9. *Your master . . . done undone:* 'Your master, either because he has changed towards me or through the mistakes of some of his officers, has given me good reason to wish that certain things had not been done.'

12. *full of regard:* quite worthy of respect.

13. *He is not doubted:* 'I have no real doubts about him.' Perhaps Brutus is modifying his criticism in the presence of Cassius's soldiers, out of respect for Cassius. If so, it would be typical of him.

16. *familiar instances:* signs of friendship.

Octavius

  Let us do so; for we are at the stake,
  And bay'd about with many enemies;
  And some that smile have in their hearts, I fear,   *50*
  Millions of mischiefs.

Exeunt

SCENE II—*The Camp near Sardis. Before the tent of Brutus*

    Drum.   Enter BRUTUS, LUCILIUS, LUCIUS, *and the*
      ARMY. TITINIUS *and* PINDARUS *meet them*

Brutus

  Stand, ho!

Lucilius

  Give the word, ho! and stand.

Brutus

  What now, Lucilius? Is Cassius near?

Lucilius

  He is at hand, and Pindarus is come
  To do you salutation from his master.   *5*

Brutus

  He greets me well. Your master, Pindarus,
  In his own change, or by ill officers,
  Hath given me some worthy cause to wish
  Things done undone; but if he be at hand
  I shall be satisfied.

Pindarus   I do not doubt   *10*
  But that my noble master will appea
  Such as he is, full of regard and honour.

Brutus

  He is not doubted. A word, Lucilius,
  How he receiv'd you; let me be resolv'd.

Lucilius

  With courtesy and with respect enough,   *15*
  But not with such familiar instances

163

17-18. *Nor with . . . of old:* 'Nor did he grant me the open and friendly conversation that he used to do some time ago.'

21. 'It resorts to a forced kind of good manners.' i.e. the bare courtesies that Lucilius received from Cassius.

23. *hollow:* false, insincere.

24. *mettle:* quality, spirit.

25. 'When they have to put up with the pain of being spurred.' In other words, 'when the going gets tough.'

26-7. *crests.* The crest was the ridge on the neck of a horse and a high crest was regarded as a sign of health and vigour.
jades: dull, feeble horses. Brutus means that these horses droop and fail when put to the test and that Cassius is like one of them.

29. *horse:* horses, cavalry.

38-9. Acutely conscious of his sense of honour and convinced that he is in the right, Brutus asks how he can possibly have wronged Cassius, his brother-in-law, when he doesn't even wrong his enemies.

Nor with such free and friendly conference
As he hath us'd of old.

Brutus   Thou hast describ'd
A hot friend cooling. Ever note, Lucilius,
When love begins to sicken and decay,   *20*
It useth an enforced ceremony.
There are no tricks in plain and simple faith;
But hollow men, like horses hot at hand,
Make gallant show and promise of their mettle;
But when they should endure the bloody spur,   *25*
They fall their crests, and like deceitful jades
Sink in the trial. Comes his army on?

Lucilius
They mean this night in Sardis to be quarter'd.
The greater part, the horse in general,
Are come with Cassius.

Low march within

Brutus   Hark! he is arriv'd: *30*
March gently on to meet him.

Enter CASSIUS *and his* POWERS

Cassius
Stand, ho!

Brutus
Stand, ho! Speak the word along.

First Soldier
Stand!

Second Soldier
Stand!   *35*

Third Soldier
Stand!

Cassius
Most noble brother, you have done me wrong.

Brutus
Judge me, you gods! wrong I mine enemies?
And, if not so, how should I wrong a brother?

165

40. *sober form:* calm and restrained manner.

42. *griefs:* grievances.
I do know you well. He probably means that Cassius is liable to get too excited in difficult moments.

46. *enlarge your griefs:* explain your grievances.

48. *charges:* troops.

50. *do you the like:* you do the same.
51. *done our conference:* finished our discussion.

SCENE III

1-5. Cassius's argument is that one of his men, Lucius Pella, was disgraced by Brutus for taking bribes from the local people and that Brutus refused to take any notice of Cassius's attempts to defend the man. This seems to be quite consistent with their personalities, Brutus idealistic and refusing to lower his moral standards; Cassius defending something corrupt but, in his opinion, of small importance in view of their dangerous situation.
2. *noted:* condemned, disgraced.
4. *praying:* pleading.
5. *slighted off:* brushed aside with contempt.

7-8. *it is not . . . comment:* 'it is wrong that every trivial fault should be criticized.'

9-10. *you yourself . . . itching palm:* 'you yourself have often been criticized for your money-grubbing (greed).'

Cassius
 Brutus, this sober form of yours hides wrongs;   *40*
 And when you do them—
Brutus   Cassius, be content;
 Speak your griefs softly; I do know you well.
 Before the eyes of both our armies here,
 Which should perceive nothing but love from us,
 Let us not wrangle. Bid them move away;   *45*
 Then in my tent, Cassius, enlarge your griefs,
 And I will give you audience.
Cassius   Pindarus,
 Bid our commanders lead their charges off
 A little from this ground.
Brutus
 Lucilius, do you the like; and let no man   *50*
 Come to our tent till we have done our conference.
 Let Lucius and Titinius guard our door.

      Exeunt

SCENE III—*The Camp near Sardis. Within the tent of Brutus*

    Enter BRUTUS *and* CASSIUS
Cassius
 That you have wrong'd me doth appear in this:
 You have condemn'd and noted Lucius Pella
 For taking bribes here of the Sardians;
 Wherein my letters, praying on his side,
 Because I knew the man, were slighted off.   *5*
Brutus
 You wrong'd yourself to write in such a case.
Cassius
 In such a time as this it is not meet
 That every nice offence should bear his comment.
Brutus
 Let me tell you, Cassius, you yourself
 Are much condemn'd to have an itching palm,   *10*

       167

11-12. *To sell . . . undeservers.* Brutus accused him of selling important offices or giving them in exchange for money, to men who had no right to them.

15-16. Cassius's reaction is anger and amazement (lines 12-14). Here, with biting sarcasm, Brutus says that Cassius seems to think he must be kept free from punishment or correction because he is such an important person.

18-21. Brutus, the idealist, always keeps in mind the principles which made him strike down Caesar. 'Justice' had not been mentioned as a motive for murdering him but it would naturally be included in Brutus's general moral beliefs.
20-1. 'Any conspirator who stabbed Caesar for any motive other than justice must have been a villain.'

23. *supporting robbers.* This is the first time we hear that Caesar had supported or tolerated thieves. It is perhaps a minor mistake that this was not mentioned before the assassination.
25-6. He means that, by accepting bribes, they would be selling not just important offices but their own honour as well. (He is probably thinking of *his* honour rather than that of Cassius). 'And sell that priceless possession, our integrity, for a fistful of coins.'
trash: a contemptuous word for 'money'.
27. *bay:* bark or howl at.
28. *bait:* harass, worry, like a dog baiting a bear. Probably the mention of 'dog' by Brutus put the idea into Cassius's mind. Some editors think that Cassius is repeating Brutus's word 'bay', in which case he means, 'Don't bark at *me*, Brutus.'
30. *hedge me in:* restrict me, tie me down. He resents having his freedom of action restricted on this question of bribery.
31. *Older in practice:* more experienced.
32. *To make conditions.* He probably means to decide the proper conditions on which to make appointments, including those that involve the exchange of money. Lines 31 and 32 are important as Brutus flings this speech back at Cassius a little later.
32. *Go to:* Nonsense! The quarrel now lapses into something little better than a 'slanging match' (a quarrel in which insults are hurled about).

36. 'Take care for your safety; don't provoke me any more.'

37. *slight:* worthless.

To sell and mart your offices for gold
To undeservers.

Cassius   I an itching palm!
You know that you are Brutus that speaks this,
Or, by the gods, this speech were else your last.

Brutus
The name of Cassius honours this corruption,   15
And chastisement doth therefore hide his head.

Cassius
Chastisement!

Brutus
Remember March, the ides of March remember:
Did not great Julius bleed for justice' sake?
What villain touch'd his body, that did stab,   20
And not for justice? What, shall one of us,
That struck the foremost man of all this world
But for supporting robbers, shall we now
Contaminate our fingers with base bribes,
And sell the mighty space of our large honours   25
For so much trash as may be grasped thus?
I had rather be a dog and bay the moon
Than such a Roman.

Cassius   Brutus, bait not me!
I'll not endure it. You forget yourself,
To hedge me in. I am a soldier, I,   30
Older in practice, abler than yourself
To make conditions.

Brutus   Go to; you are not, Cassius.

Cassius
I am.

Brutus
I say you are not.

Cassius
Urge me no more, I shall forget myself;   35
Have mind upon your health, tempt me no farther.

Brutus
Away, slight man!

38. *Is't possible?* Cassius is shocked and amazed by the harshness of Brutus's words. Brutus then demands the right to get a word in edgeways but he himself has been doing most of the talking!

39. 'Must I give free rein and scope to your fiery temper?'

40. *stares:* glares wildly (like a madman). He is referring to the angry expression on Cassius's face.

42-5. Brutus, in his anger, tells Cassius that he must vent his bad temper on slaves or other inferiors since he, Brutus, will put up with it no longer.

43. *choleric:* bad-tempered.

44. *budge:* give way.

45. *observe you:* treat you with special care and consideration.

45-8. *Must I . . . split you:* 'Do I have to put up with and grovel before your irritable moods? By heaven, you must swallow the poison of your own violent temper even if it makes you burst.'

50. *waspish:* sharp-tongued.

52. *make your vaunting true:* show that what you boast is true.

54. *learn of:* be taught by. Brutus is again being very sarcastic.

57. *Did I say 'better'?* Did he? See lines 30-2. Not exactly perhaps, but in quarrels of this kind exact meanings are likely to be forgotten in the heat of the moment.

58-64. Cassius says that not even Caesar would have dared to insult him as Brutus has done, to which Brutus replies that Cassius would never have dared to provoke Caesar. This is just general abuse on both sides, far from the original cause of their quarrel.

58. *mov'd:* roused.

59. *tempted:* see line 36.

Cassius
  Is't possible?
Brutus   Hear me, for I will speak.
  Must I give way and room to your rash choler?
  Shall I be frighted when a madman stares?   *40*
Cassius
  O ye gods, ye gods! must I endure all this?
Brutus
  All this? Ay, more! Fret till your proud heart
      break.
  Go show your slaves how choleric you are,
  And make your bondmen tremble. Must I budge?
  Must I observe you? Must I stand and crouch   *45*
  Under your testy humour? By the gods,
  You shall digest the venom of your spleen
  Though it do split you; for from this day forth
  I'll use you for my mirth, yea, for my laughter,
  When you are waspish.
Cassius   Is it come to this?   *50*
Brutus
  You say you are a better soldier.
  Let it appear so; make your vaunting true,
  And it shall please me well. For mine own part,
  I shall be glad to learn of noble men.
Cassius
  You wrong me every way; you wrong me, Brutus;   *55*
  I said an elder soldier, not a better.
  Did I say 'better'?
Brutus   If you did, I care not.
Cassius
  When Caesar liv'd, he durst not thus have mov'd me.
Brutus
  Peace, peace! You durst not so have tempted him.
Cassius
  I durst not?   *60*
Brutus
  No.

171

64-5. Cassius means that he might harm Brutus. Brutus means that Cassius has already done something he ought to be sorry for, i.e. approved or tolerated bribery.

67-9. *For I am . . . respect not:* 'For I am so well fortified by my high moral principles that your threats pass right over my head like a breath of wind that means nothing to me.' Brutus's self-righteousness becomes almost intolerable here.

71. He goes on, in the next few lines, to explain what he means by *vile means*. This is a further example of Brutus's high principles.
72-5. *I had rather . . . any indirection:* 'I would rather turn my heart into coins and pour out my blood for money than force these over-worked peasants, by unfair means, to give me their paltry pence.'

77. *Was that done like Cassius?* 'Was that the kind of thing Cassius should have done?' No doubt Brutus has had an exaggerated notion of Cassius's integrity all along.

80. *rascal counters:* wretched coins.

81-2. Brutus calls on the gods to strike him dead if *he* ever behaves in such a mean and despicable way.

85-107. During this quarrel, Cassius is deeply hurt by Brutus's harshness. He is far more emotional in this respect than his fellow-conspirator who depends far less on Cassius's friendship than Cassius does on his.
85. *riv'd:* broken.
86. *bear his friend's infirmities:* 'put up with his friend's faults and weaknesses.'

Cassius
  What, durst not tempt him?
Brutus   For your life you durst not.
Cassius
  Do not presume too much upon my love;
  I may do that I shall be sorry for.
Brutus
  You have done that you should be sorry for.   65
  There is no terror, Cassius, in your threats;
  For I am arm'd so strong in honesty
  That they pass by me as the idle wind,
  Which I respect not. I did send to you
  For certain sums of gold, which you denied me;   70
  For I can raise no money by vile means.
  By heaven, I had rather coin my heart,
  And drop my blood for drachmas, than to wring
  From the hard hands of peasants their vile trash
  By any indirection. I did send   75
  To you for gold to pay my legions,
  Which you denied me; was that done like Cassius?
  Should I have answer'd Caius Cassius so?
  When Marcus Brutus grows so covetous,
  To lock such rascal counters from his friends,   80
  Be ready, gods, with all your thunderbolts,
  Dash him to pieces!
Cassius   I denied you not.
Brutus
  You did.
Cassius   I did not. He was but a fool
  That brought my answer back.
  Brutus hath riv'd my heart.   85
  A friend should bear his friend's infirmities,
  But Brutus makes mine greater than they are.
Brutus
  I do not, till you practise them on me.
Cassius
  You love me not.

94. *alone on Cassius:* on Cassius alone.

96. *brav'd:* defied, contradicted.

97. *Check'd like a bondman:* rebuked or criticized like a servant.

98-9. *conn'd by rote . . . my teeth:* 'learned by heart to ram down my throat.'

101. *naked:* not necessarily bare, but unprotected,—i.e. without armour.

102. *Dearer than Plutus' mine:* 'more valuable than all the gold in the mine of the god of wealth.'

104. In line 82, Cassius said he did *not* refuse Brutus gold. Either he is being inconsistent under stress of emotion, or he is really saying, 'I who, *according to you*, denied you gold . . .' Oddly enough, Brutus had himself suggested offering his heart instead of gold (line 72).

105-7. Once again, Cassius in his distress turns to death as the only solution to his problems.

108. *it shall have scope:* 'it (your anger) will be allowed to express itself freely.'

109. *dishonour shall be humour:* 'I shall regard your insults as caused by moodiness.'

110-13. Brutus begins by describing himself as essentially a mild man (*lamb*), then says that his anger is really like a flint showing a brief spark when struck very hard (*much enforced*) and then returning to normal.

114. Cassius cannot forget the spitefulness of Brutus's remark (line 49).

115. 'When sorrow and his badly balanced temperament upset him.'

Brutus   I do not like your faults.
Cassius
  A friendly eye could never see such faults.   90
Brutus
  A flatterer's would not, though they do appear
  As huge as high Olympus.
Cassius
  Come, Antony, and young Octavius, come,
  Revenge yourselves alone on Cassius,
  For Cassius is aweary of the world: 95
  Hated by one he loves; brav'd by his brother;
  Check'd like a bondman; all his faults observ'd,
  Set in a notebook, learn'd, and conn'd by rote,
  To cast into my teeth. O, I could weep
  My spirit from mine eyes! There is my dagger,   100
  And here my naked breast; within, a heart
  Dearer than Plutus' mine, richer than gold;
  If that thou be'st a Roman, take it forth.
  I, that denied thee gold, will give my heart.
  Strike as thou didst at Caesar; for I know,   105
  When thou didst hate him worst, thou lov'dst him
      better
  Than ever thou lov'dst Cassius.
Brutus   Sheathe your dagger.
  Be angry when you will, it shall have scope;
  Do what you will, dishonour shall be humour.
  O Cassius, you are yoked with a lamb,   110
  That carries anger as the flint bears fire;
  Who, much enforced, shows a hasty spark,
  And straight is cold again.
Cassius   Hath Cassius liv'd
  To be but mirth and laughter to his Brutus,
  When grief and blood ill-temper'd vexeth him?   115
Brutus
  When I spoke that I was ill-temper'd too.
Cassius
  Do you confess so much? Give me your hand.

119. *bear with:* put up with, tolerate.
120. *rash humour:* violent temper.

123. *over-earnest:* too forceful or demanding.
124. *leave you so:* leave things as they are.

130-2. The poet obviously doesn't know that the generals have already settled their quarrels. The poet's rather silly lines, which happen to rhyme, provoke Cassius to laugh at him. Cassius has suffered a good deal in his dispute with Brutus and seems to find some relief for his feelings here. The more serious-minded Brutus (who, as we see later, has other anxieties on his mind) doesn't find the poet so amusing.

134. *sirrah:* fellow. *saucy:* impudent.

135. *bear with:* tolerate. *fashion:* way, custom.

136. 'I'll put up with his funny ways when he comes at the right time.'
137. *jigging:* rhyming.

Brutus
  And my heart too.
Cassius   O Brutus!
Brutus   What's the matter?
Cassius
  Have not you love enough to bear with me,
  When that rash humour which my mother gave me   *120*
  Makes me forgetful?
Brutus
  Yes, Cassius; and from henceforth,
  When you are over-earnest with your Brutus,
  He'll think your mother chides, and leave you so.

  Enter a POET, *followed by* LUCILIUS, TITINIUS, *and*
                    LUCIUS

Poet
  Let me go in to see the generals.   *125*
  There is some grudge between 'em; 'tis not meet
  They be alone.
Lucilius   You shall not come to them.
Poet
  Nothing but death shall stay me.
Cassius
  How now! What's the matter?
Poet
  For shame, you generals! What do you mean?   *130*
  Love, and be friends, as two such men should be;
  For I have seen more years, I'm sure, than ye.
Cassius
  Ha, ha! How vilely doth this cynic rhyme!
Brutus
  Get you hence, sirrah; saucy fellow, hence!
Cassius
  Bear with him, Brutus: 'tis his fashion.   *135*
Brutus
  I'll know his humour when he knows his time.
  What should the wars do with these jigging fools?

138. *Companion:* a term of contempt, 'rogue'. The exit of the poet prompts the question why Shakespeare ever brought him in. He serves no purpose in the plot of the play but he does create a slightly amusing diversion in a long and serious scene, especially as there is some even more gloomy news to come.

140. *lodge their companies:* settle down their troops.

145. The philosophy referred to here is that of the Stoics who believed that life was essentially hard and full of suffering, and that the greatest virtue was to endure it without flinching.
146. 'If you give way to misfortunes that occur by chance.'

150. The death of Portia is clearly one of the 'many griefs' that Brutus had to suffer (line 144) and would partly account for his surprisingly harsh words during the quarrel. Cassius here acknowledges this fact. 'How was it that you didn't kill me when I opposed you so sharply?'
151. *touching:* harmful, grievous.
152. *Upon what sickness?* through what illness?
154-5. *for with . . . tidings came:* 'News of the strength of Octavius and Antony came at the same time as news of her death.'
155. *fell distract:* lost her reason.
156. *swallow'd fire.* It is not clear exactly what this means, but according to Shakespeare's source, North's translation of the Roman writer Plutarch, she held hot coals in her mouth until she died.

Companion, hence!
Cassius   Away, away, be gone!

Exit POET

Brutus
　Lucilius and Titinius, bid the commanders
　Prepare to lodge their companies to-night.   *140*
Cassius
　And come yourselves, and bring Messala with you
　Immediately to us.
　　　　　　Exeunt LUCILIUS *and* TITINIUS
Brutus   Lucius, a bowl of wine!

Exit LUCIUS

Cassius
　I did not think you could have been so angry.
Brutus
　O Cassius, I am sick of many griefs!
Cassius
　Of your philosophy you make no use,   *145*
　If you give place to accidental evils.
Brutus
　No man bears sorrow better. Portia is dead.
Cassius
　Ha! Portia?
Brutus
　She is dead.
Cassius
　How scap'd I killing when I cross'd you so?   *150*
　O insupportable and touching loss!
　Upon what sickness?
Brutus   Impatient of my absence,
　And grief that young Octavius with Mark Antony
　Have made themselves so strong; for with her death
　That tidings came. With this she fell distract,   *155*
　And, her attendants absent, swallow'd fire.

179

163. *o'erswell:* overflow. Cassius feels that, if the wine in the cup is a symbol of Brutus's friendship, he can hardly drink too much of it.

172. *Bending their expedition.* directing the march of their army.

173. *self-same tenour:* exactly the same meaning.

175. *proscription·* see Act IV, Scene i, line 17.

176-7. These mass executions of the nobility of Rome re-emphasize the brutality of the new rulers.

Cassius
  And died so?
Brutus
  Even so.
Cassius
  O ye immortal gods!

          Enter LUCIUS *with wine and tapers*

Brutus
  Speak no more of her. Give me a bowl of wine.   *160*
  In this I bury all unkindness, Cassius.

                Drinks

Cassius
  My heart is thirsty for that noble pledge.
  Fill, Lucius, till the wine o'erswell the cup;
  I cannot drink too much of Brutus' love.

    Drinks.   Exit LUCIUS.   *Re-enter* TITINIUS, *with*
                    MESSALA

Brutus
  Come in, Titinius! Welcome, good Messala!   *165*
  Now sit we close about this taper here,
  And call in question our necessities.
Cassius
  Portia, art thou gone?
Brutus   No more, I pray you.
  Messala, I have here received letters,
  That young Octavius and Mark Antony   *170*
  Come down upon us with a mighty power,
  Bending their expedition toward Philippi.
Messala
  Myself have letters of the self-same tenour.
Brutus
  With what addition?
Messala
  That, by proscription and bills of outlawry,   *175*
  Octavius, Antony, and Lepidus,
  Have put to death an hundred senators.

183-97. This section refers to the death of Portia and seems to be an unnecessary repetition of the news conveyed a short while before. Most editors now feel that Shakespeare wrote this part first, felt dissatisfied with it (for reasons concerned with the character of Brutus which may be worth thinking about) and then re-wrote it as it appears in lines 147-59. The two versions were then accidentally printed together in one of the early editions and the mistake has been repeated ever since.

187. *aught:* anything.

193. *once:* at some time.

196-7. 'In theory, I have as much of this Stoical strength of character as you have, but I couldn't use it as effectively as you do.'

198. *to our work alive:* 'let us turn to work that concerns living people.'

Brutus

   Therein our letters do not well agree;
   Mine speak of seventy senators that died
   By their proscriptions, Cicero being one.   *180*

Cassius

   Cicero one!

Messala   Cicero is dead,
   And by that order of proscription.
   Had you your letters from your wife, my lord?

Brutus

   No, Messala.

Messala

   Nor nothing in your letters writ of her?   *185*

Brutus

   Nothing, Messala.

Messala   That, methinks, is strange.

Brutus

   Why ask you? Hear you aught of her in yours?

Messala

   No, my lord.

Brutus

   Now, as you are a Roman, tell me true.

Messala

   Then like a Roman bear the truth I tell: *190*
   For certain she is dead, and by strange manner.

Brutus

   Why, farewell, Portia. We must die, Messala.
   With meditating that she must die once,
   I have the patience to endure it now.

Messala

   Even so great men great losses should endure.   *195*

Cassius

   I have as much of this in art as you,
   But yet my nature could not bear it so.

Brutus

   Well, to our work alive. What do you think
   Of marching to Philippi presently?

203. *offence:* harm.

204. *defence:* ability to defend ourselves.

205. *of force:* of necessity.

207. *stand but in a forc'd affection:* have been forced to show us friendship.

208. *grudg'd us contribution:* 'given us supplies grudgingly or resentfully.'

209. *by:* through.

210. *make a fuller number up:* add to their numbers.

211-14. Brutus's plan, it seems, is to march out to meet Antony and Octavius at Philippi, thus depriving them, as he thinks, of the support and supplies which would be given them by the people round Sardis. Cassius objects but he is overruled by Brutus just as he was when he suggested (1) that the conspirators should swear an oath; (2) that Antony should be killed with Caesar and (3) when he objected to Antony speaking at Caesar's funeral. Cassius finally gives way on the present issue in line 226. One cannot help feeling that he is right on all four occasions.

217. *brim full:* fully manned. *ripe:* at its peak.

220-6. In this excellent and well-known passage, Brutus expresses his feeling that it is necessary to act quickly if they are to succeed. To understand the full meaning of the metaphor, we must remember how much the ships in Elizabethan times depended on the tides for navigating in shallow waters. The best and safest time for a merchant vessel to set out or arrive would be at about high tide, and failure to catch the tide might mean a delay of days or even weeks.

221. *flood:* at about high tide.

222-3. 'If men miss the opportunity (*tides*), the rest of their lives must be spent in difficulties and frustrations' (*shallows* and *miseries*).

226. *ventures:* cargo or merchandise. He means the cause for which they are fighting and the campaign generally.

with your will: 'since you want it that way.'

228. 'Our talk has extended well into the night.'

184

Cassius
  I do not think it good.
Brutus   Your reason?
Cassius   This it is: *200*
  'Tis better that the enemy seek us;
  So shall he waste his means, weary his soldiers,
  Doing himself offence, whilst we, lying still,
  Are full of rest, defence, and nimbleness.
Brutus
  Good reasons must, of force, give place to better.   *205*
  The people 'twixt Philippi and this ground
  Do stand but in a forc'd affection;
  For they have grudg'd us contribution.
  The enemy, marching along by them,
  By them shall make a fuller number up,   *210*
  Come on refresh'd, new-added, and encourag'd;
  From which advantage shall we cut him off,
  If at Philippi we do face him there,
  These people at our back.
Cassius   Hear me, good brother.
Brutus
  Under your pardon. You must note beside   *215*
  That we have tried the utmost of our friends,
  Our legions are brim full, our cause is ripe.
  The enemy increaseth every day:
  We, at the height, are ready to decline.
  There is a tide in the affairs of men   *220*
  Which, taken at the flood, leads on to fortune;
  Omitted, all the voyage of their life
  Is bound in shallows and in miseries.
  On such a full sea are we now afloat,
  And we must take the current when it serves,   *225*
  Or lose our ventures.
Cassius   Then, with your will, go on;
  We'll along ourselves and meet them at Philippi.
Brutus
  The deep of night is crept upon our talk,

229-30. 'And Nature demands that we should sleep, so we will grant it a small ration of rest.'

244. *o'erwatched:* overtired.

And nature must obey necessity,
Which we will niggard with a little rest.   *230*
There is no more to say?
Cassius   No more. Good night:
  Early to-morrow will we rise, and hence.
Brutus
  Lucius! [*Enter* LUCIUS]. My gown. [*Exit* LUCIUS.]
  Farewell, good Messala.
  Good night, Titinius. Noble, noble Cassius,   *235*
  Good night, and good repose!
Cassius   O my dear brother,
  This was an ill beginning of the night!
  Never come such division 'tween our souls!
  Let it not, Brutus.
Brutus   Everything is well.
Cassius
  Good night, my lord.
Brutus   Good night, good brother.   *240*
Titinius and Messala
  Good night, Lord Brutus.
Brutus   Farewell, every one.

      Exeunt CASSIUS, TITINIUS, *and* MESSALA.   *Re-enter*
                LUCIUS *with the gown*

  Give me the gown. Where is thy instrument?
Lucius
  Here in the tent.
Brutus   What, thou speak'st drowsily?
  Poor knave, I blame thee not; thou art o'erwatched.
  Call Claudius and some other of my men;   *245*
  I'll have them sleep on cushions in my tent.
Lucius
  Varro and Claudius!

              Enter VARRO *and* CLAUDIUS

250. *raise:* rouse.

254. *otherwise bethink me:* decide to do something else.

260. 'Play a few bars of music on your instrument.'

264. 'I should not try to make you do more than you are capable of doing.'
265. *young bloods:* young men.

268. *If I do live.* A phrase which could mean simply 'as long as I'm alive', but it also suggests foreboding on Brutus's part.

Varro
　　Calls my lord?
Brutus
　　I pray you, sirs, lie in my tent and sleep;
　　It may be I shall raise you by and by　　　　　　　*250*
　　On business to my brother Cassius.
Varro
　　So please you we will stand and watch your
　　　　　pleasure.
Brutus
　　I will not have it so. Lie down, good sirs;
　　It may be I shall otherwise bethink me.
　　Look, Lucius, here's the book I sought for so;　　*255*
　　I put it in the pocket of my gown.

　　　　　VARRO *and* CLAUDIUS *lie down*

Lucius
　　I was sure your lordship did not give it me.
Brutus
　　Bear with me, good boy, I am much forgetful.
　　Canst thou hold up thy heavy eyes awhile,
　　And touch thy instrument a strain or two?　　　　*260*
Lucius
　　Ay, my lord, an't please you.
Brutus　　　　　　　　　　　　It does, my boy.
　　I trouble thee too much, but thou art willing.
Lucius
　　It is my duty, sir.
Brutus
　　I should not urge thy duty past thy might;
　　I know young bloods look for a time of rest.　　　*265*
Lucius
　　I have slept, my lord, already.
Brutus
　　It was well done; and thou shalt sleep again;
　　I will not hold thee long. If I do live,
　　I will be good to thee.

270-2. Sleep is seen as a murderer who overwhelms the boy suddenly as if hitting him with a mace (a heavy metal club, used in battle); *leaden* gives the sense of heavy slumber.

278. *taper:* see Act II, Scene i, line 35. It was believed that the lights grew dim when a ghost or evil spirit appeared. To the Elizabethan audience, the appearance of Caesar's ghost to Brutus would be a clear indication that his cause was doomed to failure and that he would die.

283. *stare:* stand on end.

Music and a song. LUCIUS *falls asleep*

This is a sleepy tune. O murd'rous slumber!   270
Layest thou thy leaden mace upon my boy,
That plays thee music? Gentle knave, good night.
I will not do thee so much wrong to wake thee.
If thou dost nod, thou break'st thy instrument;
I'll take it from thee: and, good boy, good night.   275
Let me see, let me see; is not the leaf turn'd down
Where I left reading? Here it is, I think.

Sits down. Enter the GHOST *of* CAESAR

How ill this taper burns! Ha! who comes here?
I think it is the weakness of mine eyes
That shapes this monstrous apparition.   280
It comes upon me. Art thou any thing?
Art thou some god, some angel, or some devil,
That mak'st my blood cold and my hair to stare?
Speak to me what thou art.
Ghost
   Thy evil spirit, Brutus.
Brutus   Why com'st thou?   285
Ghost
   To tell thee thou shalt see me at Philippi.
Brutus
   Well; then I shall see thee again?
Ghost
   Ay, at Philippi.
Brutus
   Why, I will see thee at Philippi, then.

Exit GHOST

Now I have taken heart thou vanishest.   290
Ill spirit, I would hold more talk with thee.
Boy! Lucius! Varro! Claudius! Sirs, awake!
Claudius!
Lucius
   The strings, my lord, are false.

296-309. Brutus wakes up those around him and asks why they cried out. This must be because he wants to make quite sure that he did in fact see and hear a ghost. If one of the others had cried out in his sleep, Brutus hopes that that might account for what he heard but it seems that they had all been sleeping soundly.

310. 'Tell him to march off his troops early before me.'

Brutus
  He thinks he still is at his instrument.   295
  Lucius, awake!
Lucius
  My lord!
Brutus
  Didst thou dream, Lucius, that thou so criedst out?
Lucius
  My lord, I do not know that I did cry.
Brutus
  Yes, that thou didst. Didst thou see any thing?   300
Lucius
  Nothing, my lord.
Brutus
  Sleep again, Lucius. Sirrah Claudius!
  [*To* VARRO]. Fellow thou, awake!
Varro
  My lord?
Claudius
  My lord?   305
Brutus
  Why did you so cry out, sirs, in your sleep?
Both
  Did we, my lord?
Brutus   Ay. Saw you any thing?
Varro
  No, my lord, I saw nothing.
Claudius   Nor I, my lord.
Brutus
  Go and commend me to my brother Cassius;
  Bid him set on his pow'rs betimes before,   310
  And we will follow.
Varro and Claudius
  It shall be done, my lord.

Exeunt

The inevitable battle is finally joined but not before the main issues and characters of the play are, as it were, summed up for our reconsideration and re-assessment in a parley. In a few brief but revealing words, each person again shows us what he thinks and what his character is but, in contrast to the aggressive confidence shown by Antony and Octavius, Brutus and Cassius are brooding and uncertain, though still determined.

1. *our hopes are answered:* 'That's just what we wanted.' Poor Brutus, by insisting on marching straight to Philippi, has done exactly what his enemies hoped he would do.

4. *battles:* armies.

5. *warn:* challenge.

6. He means that their enemies are offering defiance before they have been threatened.

7. *in their bosoms:* 'I know what they are thinking.' The *Tut* indicates Antony's irritation. He had predicted that the conspirators would wait in the hills and doesn't like being told by Octavius that he was wrong.

8. *Wherefore:* why.

8-11. *They could be . . . have courage:* 'They would be only too happy to be somewhere else, but they have come down with a display of courage to mask their fear, thinking by this deception to persuade us that they are brave men.'

10. *fearful bravery.* 'Fearful' can mean 'full of fear' and 'causing fear'. 'Bravery' can mean 'bravado' and 'finery'. Probably all these meanings are intended here.

14. *bloody sign of battle.* A red flag was the Roman signal for battle.

16-18. The command of the right flank was the position of greater honour and responsibility in the Roman army.

16. *softly:* gently, slowly.

17. *even field:* level plain.

ACT FIVE

Enter OCTAVIUS, ANTONY, *and their* ARMY

Octavius
  Now, Antony, our hopes are answered.
  You said the enemy would not come down,
  But keep the hills and upper regions;
  It proves not so. Their battles are at hand;
  They mean to warn us at Philippi here,   *5*
  Answering before we do demand of them.

Antony
  Tut, I am in their bosoms, and I know
  Wherefore they do it. They could be content
  To visit other places, and come down
  With fearful bravery, thinking by this face   *10*
  To fasten in our thoughts that they have courage;
  But 'tis not so.

Enter a MESSENGER

Messenger   Prepare you, generals:
  The enemy comes on in gallant show;
  Their bloody sign of battle is hung out,
  And something to be done immediately.   *15*

Antony
  Octavius, lead your battle softly on,
  Upon the left hand of the even field.

Octavius
  Upon the right hand I: keep thou the left.

Antony
  Why do you cross me in this exigent?

20. 'I do not wish to oppose you, but I will do what I have said.'

24. He intends to wait and let the enemy attack first.

27-9. Brutus as we have seen is not really a man of action. He prefers to think, reflect and read. Perhaps this is the reason for his errors in practical matters.

30. *bad strokes.* Brutus had meant the sword-thrusts of the coming battle when he used these words but Antony makes them apply to the stabbing of Caesar by Brutus when the conspirators spoke flatteringly to Caesar.

33. 'We don't know yet what sort of strokes *you* are going to give.'

34-5. *But for . . . honeyless.* Hybla was a place in Sicily famous for its honey. Cassius means that Antony can speak very sweetly when he wants to. Perhaps he is referring to Antony's forum speech or his words when he made his agreement with the conspirators. More likely, he is being sarcastic at the expense of Antony's very blunt words to Brutus lines (21-2).

35. The mention of bees makes Antony suggest that he has taken the stings of the bees as well as their honey. This is a grim reminder that he and his troops have swords.

39-44. Antony now drops this game of words and speaks directly and passionately, expressing his disgust at the murder of Caesar.

Octavius

  I do not cross you; but I will do so.   *20*

    March. Drum. Enter BRUTUS, CASSIUS, *and their*
    ARMY; LUCILIUS, TITINIUS, MESSALA, *and* OTHERS

Brutus

  They stand, and would have parley.

Cassius

  Stand fast, Titinius; we must out and talk.

Octavius

  Mark Antony, shall we give sign of battle?

Antony

  No, Caesar, we will answer on their charge.

  Make forth; the generals would have some words.   *25*

Octavius

  Stir not until the signal.

Brutus

  Words before blows. Is it so, countrymen?

Octavius

  Not that we love words better, as you do.

Brutus

  Good words are better than bad strokes, Octavius.

Antony

  In your bad strokes, Brutus, you give good words;   *30*

  Witness the hole you made in Caesar's heart,

  Crying 'Long live! Hail, Caesar!'

Cassius   Antony,

  The posture of your blows are yet unknown;

  But for your words, they rob the Hybla bees,

  And leave them honeyless.

Antony   Not stingless too?   *35*

Brutus

  O yes, and soundless too;

  For you have stol'n their buzzing, Antony,

  And very wisely threat before you sting.

Antony

  Villains, you did not so when your vile daggers

41. *show'd your teeth.* This refers to the flattering smiles the murderers displayed immediately before stabbing Caesar.

41-3. *apes . . . hounds . . . cur.* These comparisons with animals all indicate Antony's scorn and hatred.

46-7. *This tongue . . . have rul'd:* 'Antony would not have been alive today to utter these words if I had had my way.'

48. *the cause:* 'come to the point.' The young and impatient Octavius has no time for this backchat.

48-9. *If arguing . . . redder drops:* 'If we work up a sweat doing nothing more strenuous than argue, then fighting will certainly lead to bloodshed.'

proof: test, demonstration.

52. *goes up:* goes back into its sheath.

54-5. *or till . . . traitors:* 'or until you traitors have killed another Caesar (i.e. myself)'.

56-7. Brutus resents Octavius's accusation that he is a traitor. He says here that Octavius can only be killed by a traitor if there is a traitor among his own followers since the 'true Romans' are the conspirators. Perhaps he means that, to be killed by a traitor, Octavius must kill himself.

59. *strain:* breed, family.

60. *honourable:* honourably. Brutus's amazingly self-satisfied reply shows what a high opinion he has of himself.

61-2. The *peevish schoolboy* is the youngster Octavius; the *masker and the reveller* is Antony. A masque was a kind of play. Both these comments tell some truth about the two characters they attempt to describe but they also show Cassius's bitter and vindictive nature.

66. *When you have stomachs:* 'When you feel like it.' (Compare the modern slang 'If you've got the guts for it.')

Hack'd one another in the sides of Caesar.　　　　**40**
You show'd your teeth like apes, and fawn'd like
　　hounds,
And bow'd like bondmen, kissing Caesar's feet;
Whilst damned Casca, like a cur, behind
Struck Caesar on the neck. O you flatterers!

Cassius

Flatterers! Now, Brutus, thank yourself:　　　　**45**
This tongue had not offended so to-day
If Cassius might have rul'd.

Octavius

Come, come, the cause. If arguing make us sweat,
The proof of it will turn to redder drops.
Look,　　　　**50**
I draw a sword against conspirators;
When think you that the sword goes up again?
Never till Caesar's three and thirty wounds
Be well aveng'd, or till another Caesar
Have added slaughter to the sword of traitors.　　　　**55**

Brutus

Caesar, thou canst not die by traitors' hands,
Unless thou bring'st them with thee.

Octavius　　　　　　　　　　So I hope.
I was not born to die on Brutus' sword.

Brutus

O, if thou wert the noblest of thy strain,
Young man, thou couldst not die more honourable.　　**60**

Cassius

A peevish schoolboy, worthless of such honour,
Join'd with a masker and a reveller!

Antony

Old Cassius still!

Octavius　　　　　　Come, Antony; away!
Defiance, traitors, hurl we in your teeth.
If you dare fight to-day, come to the field;　　　　**65**
If not, when you have stomachs.

67. These expressions show Cassius's anxiety about the coming 'storm' of battle. 'Let the wind blow, the waves rise and the ship sail as best it can.'

68. *all is on the hazard:* everything is at stake.

72. *as:* on.

75-6. *am I compelled . . . liberties:* 'I have been forced to risk all our fortunes on one battle.' Pompey had been persuaded to do the same in his last battle against Caesar.

77. *held Epicurus strong:* strongly believed in Epicurus's ideas. The Epicurean philosophy, unlike the Stoic, generally said that life could and should be enjoyed. One particular detail of its belief was that omens had no significance. Cassius here says that his faith in his philosophy has been shaken.

79. 'And half believe in the significance of portents and omens.'

80. *former:* foremost; the ensign in the vanguard of the marching army.

81. *eagles.* Eagles have usually been regarded as dominant and powerful among birds and thus signify good fortune.

fell: flew down and settled.

83. *consorted:* escorted.

85. *ravens, crows, and kites.* These are all birds of bad omen partly, no doubt, because, unlike eagles, they do not kill their own prey but feed on what they find dead. The thought behind Cassius's words is that these birds are waiting until after the battle when they will feed on the corpses of the army they are following.

87. *As:* as if.

90-2. *I but believe it partly:* 'I do not wholly believe it.' Cassius struggles not to give way to despair but his sense of foreboding cannot really be overcome.

Exeunt OCTAVIUS, ANTONY, *and their* ARMY

Cassius
  Why, now, blow wind, swell billow, and swim bark!
  The storm is up, and all is on the hazard.
Brutus
  Ho, Lucilius! hark, a word with you.
Lucilius
  My lord.   70

BRUTUS *and* LUCILIUS *converse apart*

Cassius
  Messala.
Messala   What says my general?
Cassius   Messala,
  This is my birth-day; as this very day
  Was Cassius born. Give me thy hand, Messala.
  Be thou my witness that against my will,
  As Pompey was, am I compell'd to set   75
  Upon one battle all our liberties.
  You know that I held Epicurus strong,
  And his opinion; now I change my mind,
  And partly credit things that do presage.
  Coming from Sardis, on our former ensign   80
  Two mighty eagles fell; and there they perch'd,
  Gorging and feeding from our soldiers' hands,
  Who to Philippi here consorted us.
  This morning are they fled away and gone,
  And in their steads do ravens, crows, and kites,   85
  Fly o'er our heads and downward look on us
  As we were sickly prey. Their shadows seem
  A canopy most fatal, under which
  Our army lies, ready to give up the ghost.
Messala
  Believe not so.
Cassius   I but believe it partly;   90
  For I am fresh of spirit and resolv'd
  To meet all perils very constantly.

94. *The gods . . . friendly:* 'May the gods help us.'

96. *rest still incertain:* always remain uncertain.
97. 'Let us consider the worst thing that can happen to us.'

101-2. Brutus says that he will act in accordance with the Stoic philosophy, which condemned suicide, just as he had disapproved of Cato (his uncle and father-in-law) for committing suicide. Cato is only mentioned on one other occasion in the play (Act II, Scene i, line 295.)

105-8. *so to . . . us below.* Brutus says it is cowardly to cut short his span of life in such a way; his philosophy is to prepare himself to face up to the fate ordained by the gods who rule over our lives on earth.

111. Brutus here seems inconsistent and, as we see later, he does in fact kill himself. One explanation for this is that Brutus's philosophy conflicts with the realization of what his fate will be if he is captured and that the grim reality of his position persuades him to give up his life's philosophy in his last moments. This is probably true but we must always remember how Shakespeare in this play has consistently used various signs to indicate to the audience what is to come. Cassius has wavered in his philosophy and recovered it rather unconvincingly; here Brutus also wavers. Shakespeare's intention seems clear—the conspirators are doomed and in their hearts they know it.
113. *He bears too great a mind:* 'He is too proud.' True enough!
116-22. These are hardly the words of generals confident of victory.
119. 'If we do not meet again, then we will have said our farewells already.'

Brutus
  Even so, Lucilius.
Cassius   Now, most noble Brutus,
  The gods to-day stand friendly, that we may,
  Lovers in peace, lead on our days to age!   95
  But, since the affairs of men rest still incertain,
  Let's reason with the worst that may befall.
  If we do lose this battle, then is this
  The very last time we shall speak together.
  What are you then determined to do?   100
Brutus
  Even by the rule of that philosophy
  By which I did blame Cato for the death
  Which he did give himself—I know not how,
  But I do find it cowardly and vile,
  For fear of what might fall, so to prevent   105
  The time of life—arming myself with patience
  To stay the providence of some high powers
  That govern us below.
Cassius   Then, if we lose this battle,
  You are contented to be led in triumph
  Through the streets of Rome?   110
Brutus
  No, Cassius, no. Think not, thou noble Roman,
  That ever Brutus will go bound to Rome;
  He bears too great a mind. But this same day
  Must end that work the ides of March begun,
  And whether we shall meet again I know not.   115
  Therefore our everlasting farewell take:
  For ever and for ever farewell, Cassius!
  If we do meet again, why, we shall smile;
  If not, why then this parting was well made.
Cassius
  For ever and for ever farewell, Brutus!   120
  If we do meet again, we'll smile indeed;
  If not, 'tis true this parting was well made.

123-5. Brutus goes into battle in a state of uncertainty.

SCENE II

Though the outcome of the battle can hardly be in doubt, the reasons for the victory of Caesar's forces are significant. The skill and generalship of Octavius and Antony are hardly referred to—only the errors and follies of their opponents. Brutus, as he has done before, makes blunders of judgment; Cassius's death is tragically the result of a misunderstanding. One cannot help feeling that they are haunted, as indeed they are, quite literally, as Shakespeare again makes clear at the separate deaths of the friends. The gloom and misery of these last scenes are relieved to some extent by several examples of human virtue—loyalty, courage, magnanimity and sincere tributes paid to dead friends and enemies.

1. *bills:* written orders.

3. *set on:* attack.

4. *cold demeanour . . . wing:* 'a faint-hearted attitude amongst Octavius's troops.' These troops, as Octavius insisted (see Act V, Scene i, line 18), were fighting on their right wing, opposing Brutus, who commanded the left wing of his own army.

6. Brutus thinks that an immediate assault by the whole army will win the battle for them.

SCENE III

2. *Myself . . . enemy:* 'I have become the enemy of my own troops' (by killing the ensign).

3. *ensign:* standard-bearer.

5-8. Brutus can be criticized for attacking too soon and for allowing his soldiers to waste time plundering the enemy camp. But his troops were, in fact, successful, whereas Cassius's were not and the only way

Brutus

Why then, lead on. O that a man might know
The end of this day's business ere it come!
But it sufficeth that the day will end,   *125*
And then the end is known. Come, ho! away!

Exeunt

SCENE II—*Near Philippi.   The field of battle*

Alarum.   Enter BRUTUS *and* MESSALA

Brutus

Ride, ride, Messala, ride, and give these bills
Unto the legions on the other side.

Loud alarum

Let them set on at once; for I perceive
But cold demeanour in Octavius' wing,
And sudden push gives them the overthrow.   *5*
Ride, ride, Messala; let them all come down.

Exeunt

SCENE III—*Another part of the field*

Alarums.   Enter CASSIUS *and* TITINIUS

Cassius

O, look, Titinius, look, the villains fly!
Myself have to mine own turn'd enemy.
This ensign here of mine was turning back;
I slew the coward, and did take it from him.

Titinius

O Cassius, Brutus gave the word too early,   *5*
Who, having some advantage on Octavius,

205

Cassius could stop the panic amongst his own soldiers was by the ruthless action of killing his own standard-bearer. Perhaps Cassius didn't command enough respect or authority to make his men stand firm by any other method?

15. *hide thy spurs:* 'dig your spurs in deeply,' i.e. ride as fast as you can.

19. *even with a thought:* in a flash, as quick as thought.

21. *thick:* poor, dim. *regard:* look, observe.
22. *what thou not'st:* what you see.

25. *My life . . . compass:* 'My life has completed its span.' Cassius is convinced that his death is near.

29. *on the spur.* The men spur their horses towards Titinius.

Took it too eagerly. His soldiers fell to spoil,
Whilst we by Antony are all enclos'd.

Enter PINDARUS

Pindarus
Fly further off, my lord, fly further off;
Mark Antony is in your tents, my lord;   10
Fly, therefore, noble Cassius, fly far off.
Cassius
This hill is far enough. Look, look, Titinius.
Are those my tents where I perceive the fire?
Titinius
They are, my lord.
Cassius   Titinius, if thou lovest me,
Mount thou my horse and hide thy spurs in him,   15
Till he have brought thee up to yonder troops
And here again, that I may rest assur'd
Whether yond troops are friend or enemy.
Titinius
I will be here again even with a thought.

Exit

Cassius
Go, Pindarus, get higher on that hill;   20
My sight was ever thick; regard Titinius,
And tell me what thou not'st about the field.

PINDARUS *goes up*

This day I breathed first. Time is come round,
And where I did begin there shall I end;
My life is run his compass. Sirrah, what news?   25
Pindarus
[*Above*] O my lord!
Cassius
What news?
Pindarus
Titinius is enclosed round about
With horsemen that make to him on the spur;

31. *light:* dismount.

32. *ta'en:* taken, captured.

38. *I swore . . . life:* 'I swore to you, having spared your life.'

41-2. *be a freeman . . . bosom.* He means that, by killing Cassius, Pindarus will be freed from bondage to his master.

43. *hilts:* hilt.

46. Notice the ironical fact that Cassius kills himself with the sword that killed Caesar. The spirit of Caesar, in spite of the conspirators' efforts, is still very much alive.

48. *Durst . . . will:* 'If I had dared act as I wanted to.' He means that he would rather not have killed Cassius; perhaps that he would have preferred to kill himself.

Yet he spurs on. Now they are almost on him.   *30*
Now Titinius! Now some light. O, he lights too!
He's ta'en.

Shout

And hark! They shout for joy.

Cassius

Come down; behold no more.
O, coward that I am to live so long
To see my best friend ta'en before my face!   *35*

Enter PINDARUS

Come hither, sirrah.
In Parthia did I take thee prisoner;
And then I swore thee, saving of thy life,
That whatsoever I did bid thee do
Thou shouldst attempt it. Come now, keep thine
        oath;   *40*
Now be a freeman, and with this good sword,
That ran through Caesar's bowels, search this bosom.
Stand not to answer; here, take thou the hilts;
And when my face is cover'd, as 'tis now,
Guide thou the sword.

PINDARUS *stabs him*

                Caesar, thou art reveng'd,   *45*
Even with the sword that kill'd thee.

Dies

Pindarus

So, I am free; yet would not so have been,
Durst I have done my will. O Cassius!
Far from this country Pindarus shall run,
Where never Roman shall take note of him.   *50*

Exit. Re-enter TITINIUS, *with* MESSALA

51. *It is but change.* This refers to the alternating fortunes of the battle.

58. *O my heart!* He feels his heart miss a beat as he suddenly realizes what must have happened to Cassius.

59. With emphasis on 'was'.

60-2. This vivid simile reminds us of the many other references to blood in the play and the theme of death that prompts them. Here, Cassius is described in perhaps undeservedly glowing terms. Note that, according to line 109, it is only three o'clock, but this minor inconsistency need not bother anybody in the theatre. Time is often compressed in this way in drama, especially by Shakespeare.

64. Anything damp, such as clouds, dew, fog, etc., was regarded by Shakespeare as unhealthy.

65. 'Fears about the results (of my reconnaissance) caused Cassius to do this.'

success: result, outcome.

67-71. 'Error' is seen as the offspring of depression causing men to be deceived. As soon as it comes into being it kills its 'parents', in this case Cassius, who made the original error of thinking that Titinius had been captured. Cassius's melancholy might be regarded as part of his character (in keeping with Caesar's description of him as appearing 'lean and hungry' Act I, Scene ii, line 195) or, more likely, it might be a result of the influence of Caesar's spirit which was leading him to destruction.

68. *apt:* ready (i.e. to be deceived.)

Messala
　It is but change, Titinius; for Octavius
　Is overthrown by noble Brutus' power,
　As Cassius' legions are by Antony.
Titinius
　These tidings will well comfort Cassius.
Messala
　Where did you leave him?
Titinius　　　　　　　　All disconsolate,　　　　　　55
　With Pindarus, his bondman, on this hill.
Messala
　Is not that he that lies upon the ground?
Titinius
　He lies not like the living. O my heart!
Messala
　Is not that he?
Titinius　　　　No, this was he, Messala;
　But Cassius is no more. O setting sun,　　　　　　60
　As in thy red rays thou dost sink to-night,
　So in his red blood Cassius' day is set!
　The sun of Rome is set. Our day is gone;
　Clouds, dews, and dangers come; our deeds are done.
　Mistrust of my success hath done this deed.　　　65
Messala
　Mistrust of good success hath done this deed.
　O hateful error, melancholy's child,
　Why dost thou show to the apt thoughts of men
　The things that are not? O error, soon conceiv'd,
　Thou never com'st unto a happy birth,　　　　　70
　But kill'st the mother that engender'd thee!
Titinius
　What, Pindarus! Where art thou, Pindarus?
Messala
　Seek him, Titinius, whilst I go to meet
　The noble Brutus, thrusting this report
　Into his ears. I may say 'thrusting' it;　　　　　75
　For piercing steel and darts envenomed

78. *Hie you:* hurry.

84. *misconstrued:* misunderstood.
85. *hold thee:* wait.

89-90. Titinius begs pardon of the gods for ending his life prematurely, not awaiting their decision about when he should die. He claims that it is a Roman's privilege and duty to do this on such an occasion.

94-6. Brutus explicitly states what he already knows—that Caesar's spirit is not really dead.

96. *proper:* own (Brutus is repeating himself to give emphasis to what he says).

97. *whe'r:* whether.

Shall be as welcome to the ears of Brutus
As tidings of this sight.
Titinius   Hie you, Messala,
And I will seek for Pindarus the while.

Exit MESSALA

Why didst thou send me forth, brave Cassius?   *80*
Did I not meet thy friends, and did not they
Put on my brows this wreath of victory,
And bid me give it thee? Didst thou not hear their
    shouts?
Alas, thou hast misconstrued every thing!
But hold thee, take this garland on thy brow;   *85*
Thy Brutus bid me give it thee, and I
Will do his bidding. Brutus, come apace,
And see how I regarded Caius Cassius,
By your leave, gods. This is a Roman's part.
Come, Cassius' sword, and find Titinius' heart.   *90*

Dies.   Alarum.   Re-enter MESSALA, *with* BRUTUS,
YOUNG CATO, STRATO, VOLUMNIUS, *and* LUCILIUS

Brutus
Where, where, Messala, doth his body lie?
Messala
Lo yonder, and Titinius mourning it.
Brutus
Titinius' face is upward.
Cato   He is slain.
Brutus
O Julius Caesar , thou art mighty yet!
Thy spirit walks abroad and turns our swords   *95*
In our own proper entrails.

Low alarums

Cato   Brave Titinius!
Look whe'r he have not crown'd dead Cassius!

99-103. Cassius again receives a very flattering tribute from one of his fellow-conspirators.

103. He means that he will find time later to mourn Cassius's death properly.

105-6. Like a good general, Brutus is anxious not to lower the morale of his men by having a funeral procession in the camp while the outcome of the battle is still in doubt. He shows similar concern for the spirit of his men in Act IV, Scene ii, lines 43-5, when he tells Cassius that they shouldn't squabble in front of their troops..
106. *discomfort:* dishearten.
108. *battles:* armies.

SCENE IV

2. *What bastard doth not?* 'Who is so vile that he will not?'

7-8. Some editors think Shakespeare meant these lines to be spoken by Lucilius. Clearly, Lucilius pretends to be Brutus in line 14 and it would suit the situation very well for him to begin his speech two lines earlier.

Brutus

Are yet two Romans living such as these?
The last of all the Romans, fare thee well!
It is impossible that ever Rome   *100*
Should breed thy fellow. Friends, I owe moe tears
To this dead man than you shall see me pay.
I shall find time, Cassius, I shall find time.
Come, therefore, and to Thasos send his body.
His funerals shall not be in our camp,   *105*
Lest it discomfort us. Lucilius, come;
And come, young Cato; let us to the field.
Labeo and Flavius set our battles on.
'Tis three o'clock; and, Romans, yet ere night
We shall try fortune in a second fight.

Exeunt

SCENE IV—*Another part of the field*

Alarum.   Enter BRUTUS, MESSALA, YOUNG CATO,
LUCILIUS, *and* FLAVIUS

Brutus

Yet, countrymen, O, yet hold up your heads!
Cato

What bastard doth not? Who will go with me?
I will proclaim my name about the field:
I am the son of Marcus Cato, ho!
A foe to tyrants, and my country's friend.   *5*
I am the son of Marcus Cato, ho!

Enter SOLDIERS *and fight*

Brutus

And I am Brutus, Marcus Brutus, I!
Brutus, my country's friend! Know me for Brutus!

Exit. YOUNG CATO *falls*

215

15. *A noble prisoner.* Such a prisoner would be better taken alive than dead, both for the ransom and perhaps for the triumph and glory of 'showing off' an enemy leader.

24. *or . . . or:* 'either . . . or', as usual in Shakespeare.
25. *like himself:* as he really is, i.e. true to his honourable nature.

26-9. Antony here praises Lucilius for his courage and loyalty in doing his best to protect his commander.

30. *whe'r:* whether.

32. *is chanc'd:* has turned out, happened.

Lucilius
  O young and noble Cato, art thou down?
  Why, now thou diest as bravely as Titinius,   *10*
  And mayst be honour'd, being Cato's son.
First Soldier
  Yield, or thou diest.
Lucilius   Only I yield to die.
  [*Offering money*] There is so much that thou wilt
    kill me straight.
  Kill Brutus, and be honour'd in his death.
First Soldier
  We must not. A noble prisoner!   *15*

           Enter ANTONY

Second Soldier
  Room, ho! Tell Antony Brutus is ta'en.
First Soldier
  I'll tell the news. Here comes the general.
  Brutus is ta'en! Brutus is ta'en, my lord!
Antony
  Where is he?
Lucilius
  Safe, Antony; Brutus is safe enough.   *20*
  I dare assure thee that no enemy
  Shall ever take alive the noble Brutus.
  The gods defend him from so great a shame!
  When you do find him, or alive or dead,
  He will be found like Brutus, like himself.   *25*
Antony
  This is not Brutus, friend; but, I assure you,
  A prize no less in worth. Keep this man safe;
  Give him all kindness. I had rather have
  Such men my friends than enemies. Go on,
  And see whe'r Brutus be alive or dead;   *30*
  And bring us word unto Octavius' tent
  How everything is chanc'd.

          Exeunt

SCENE V

2-3. These lines can only be explained by reference to Plutarch. From him we learn that Statilius tried to find a way to the camp to see how many men had survived the battle. If all was well, he was to show a light. But his failure to return is the end of Brutus's hopes.

4. *Slaying is the word.* He means that many people have been killed or committed suicide, with a hint that others must die too, particularly himself.

13. *vessel.* Literally, something that contains something else, especially a liquid; in this way, the body is a 'vessel' for the soul. Here, the reference is to Brutus himself who is so full of grief that he 'overflows' in tears.

SCENE V—*Another part of the field*

Enter BRUTUS, DARDANIUS, CLITUS, STRATO, *and*
VOLUMNIUS

Brutus
  Come, poor remains of friends, rest on this rock.
Clitus
  Statilius show'd the torch-light; but, my lord,
  He came not back. He is or ta'en or slain.
Brutus
  Sit thee down, Clitus. Slaying is the word;
  It is a deed in fashion. Hark thee, Clitus.   5

                    Whispering

Clitus
  What, I, my lord? No, not for all the world.
Brutus
  Peace, then, no words.
Clitus   I'll rather kill myself.
Brutus
  Hark thee, Dardanius!
Dardanius   Shall I do such a deed?
Clitus
  O Dardanius!
Dardanius
  O Clitus!   10
Clitus
  What ill request did Brutus make to thee?
Dardanius
  To kill him, Clitus. Look, he meditates.
Clitus
  Now is that noble vessel full of grief,
  That it runs over even at his eyes.
Brutus
  Come hither, good Volumnius; list a word.   15

18. *several:* separate, different. So the ghost of Caesar kept his word! (See Act IV, Scene iii, line 286).

22. *the world . . . goes:* what the indications are; what our fate is to be.
23. *pit.* Animals were sometimes hunted by being driven towards a large hole, dug as a trap. The idea of a grave is also suggested by this word.

25. *tarry:* wait.

28. *hilts:* hilt (after all, there are two sections of a sword-hilt).

29. *office:* duty.

30. *there is no tarrying here:* 'It is too dangerous to linger here.'

32-3. Strato has been asleep, presumably through exhaustion after the battle, and therefore doesn't know what Brutus and the others have been talking about.
33-8. These lines reveal a good deal about Brutus. Firstly, the fact that all his followers have been loyal to him to the bitter end seems to be true and this shows Brutus's nobility in that he has inspired such loyalty. His belief that he will gain glory in *losing* the battle seems odd at first, but he probably means that it is better to be defeated fighting for a good cause than to triumph in an evil one. No doubt his description of his enemies' conquest as *vile* is based on his belief, still firmly held, that the triumph of Caesar's cause is a black day for Rome and that in due course all true Romans will realize this.
41-2. *my bones . . . hour:* 'my body, having lived and worked simply for this end, now wishes to rest.' By this, Brutus is not likely to have meant that he has failed; rather, it is a Stoical acceptance of his fate.

Volumnius
  What says my lord?
Brutus   Why, this, Volumnius:
  The ghost of Caesar hath appear'd to me
  Two several times by night—at Sardis once,
  And this last night here in Philippi fields.
  I know my hour is come.
Volumnius   Not so, my lord.   20
Brutus
  Nay, I am sure it is, Volumnius.
  Thou seest the world, Volumnius, how it goes:
  Our enemies have beat us to the pit;

                    Low alarums

  It is more worthy to leap in ourselves
  Than tarry till they push us. Good Volumnius,   25
  Thou know'st that we two went to school together;
  Even for that our love of old, I prithee,
  Hold thou my sword-hilts whilst I run on it.
Volumnius
  That's not an office for a friend, my lord.

                    Alarum still

Clitus
  Fly, fly, my lord; there is no tarrying here.   30
Brutus
  Farewell to you; and you; and you, Volumnius.
  Strato, thou hast been all this while asleep;
  Farewell to thee too, Strato. Countrymen,
  My heart doth joy that yet in all my life
  I found no man but he was true to me.   35
  I shall have glory by this losing day,
  More than Octavius and Mark Antony
  By this vile conquest shall attain unto.
  So fare you well at once; for Brutus' tongue
  Hath almost ended his life's history.   40
  Night hangs upon mine eyes; my bones would rest,
  That have but labour'd to attain this hour.

45. *of a good respect:* held in high regard.

46. 'Your life has had its honourable side.

50-1. There is now no need for Caesar's ghost to go 'ranging for revenge' (see Act III, Scene i, line 271).

54. *bondage.* Presumably this refers to the 'bondage' of still being alive.

55. They can only put his body on a funeral pyre.

59. *Lucilius's saying.* He had said that Brutus would be found 'like Brutus, like himself.' (Act V, Scene iv, line 25.)

60. *entertain.* He will take them into his service.

Alarum. Cry within 'Fly, fly, fly!'

Clitus
  Fly, my lord, fly.
Brutus   Hence! I will follow.

          Exeunt CLITUS, DARDANIUS, *and* VOLUMNIUS

  I prithee, Strato, stay thou by thy lord;
  Thou art a fellow of a good respect;   *45*
  Thy life hath had some smatch of honour in it.
  Hold then my sword, and turn away thy face,
  While I do run upon it. Wilt thou, Strato?
Strato
  Give me your hand first. Fare you well, my lord.
Brutus
  Farewell, good Strato. Caesar, now be still.   *50*
  I kill'd not thee with half so good a will.

          He runs on his sword, and dies

     Alarum.   Retreat.   Enter OCTAVIUS, ANTONY,
          MESSALA, LUCILIUS, *and the* ARMY

Octavius
  What man is that?
Messala
  My master's man. Strato, where is thy master?
Strato
  Free from the bondage you are in, Messala.
  The conquerors can but make a fire of him;   *55*
  For Brutus only overcame himself,
  And no man else hath honour by his death.
Lucilius
  So Brutus should be found. I thank thee, Brutus,
  That thou hast prov'd Lucilius' saying true.
Octavius
  All that serv'd Brutus, I will entertain them.   *60*
  Fellow, wilt thou bestow thy time with me?

62. *prefer:* recommend.

67. *latest:* last. Aiding Brutus to kill himself is thus regarded as a 'service' to him.

68-75. This famous tribute to Brutus, uttered by his enemy, must surely be accepted as fair and just comment.

71-2. *in a general honest . . . to all:* 'sincerely believing that what he did was for the good of the people.'

73. *gentle:* noble. *elements:* qualities. Strictly speaking, 'humours', i.e. basic substances of which the body was made and which, in the right proportions, produced the perfect man.

76. *use:* treat.

77. *burial.* This refers to funeral rites generally, since the Romans normally cremated their dead—as suggested by line 55.

79. *ordered honourably:* treated with dignity and respect.

81. *part:* share out.

Strato

  Ay, if Messala will prefer me to you.

Octavius

  Do so, good Messala.

Messala

  How died my master, Strato?

Strato

  I held the sword, and he did run on it.   65

Messala

  Octavius, then take him to follow thee,

  That did the latest service to my master.

Antony

  This was the noblest Roman of them all.

  All the conspirators save only he

  Did that they did in envy of great Caesar;   70

  He only in a general honest thought

  And common good to all made one of them.

  His life was gentle; and the elements

  So mix'd in him that Nature might stand up

  And say to all the world 'This was a man!'   75

Octavius

  According to his virtue let us use him,

  With all respect and rites of burial.

  Within my tent his bones to-night shall lie,

  Most like a soldier, ordered honourably.

  So call the field to rest, and let's away   80

  To part the glories of this happy day.

Exeunt

SUMMING UP

There are many ways of reading and enjoying Shakespeare and *Julius Caesar* may be appreciated by various people in widely different ways. Some see it as a study of human character, particularly in situations of stress or conflict; others regard it as a fairly simple story of murder and revenge. The construction of the drama, the conflicting ideologies, the political interest and the language may all appeal in their way to different readers and audiences. All these elements are there, no doubt, and others, but it is the job of a critic to seek the whole truth, not just part of it, and though it may be rash to be too emphatic in our conclusions, a final judgment must obviously take into account all aspects.

But first it may be best to urge the reader to enjoy the play for its quite simple and obvious merits. The skill with which Cassius works on Brutus; Caesar's amazement when he sees that his friend Brutus is amongst those who stab him; the electric tension after the murder; Antony's remarkable oratory and the crowd's frenzy; the bitter quarrel between Brutus and Cassius; the haunting presence of Caesar, even more powerful after his death than before – all these are examples of fine dramatic writing and we would do well to appreciate and enjoy them for what they are without resorting to analysis for deeper understanding.

However, analysis, properly applied, can lead to greater understanding and the simplest and most popular analytical approach to the play lies through the characters in it. Here, differences of opinion and controversy will inevitably arise and the reader must remember to seek Shakespeare's intention rather than search for justification of his own opinion. In the case of Caesar, for example, it is really impossible to leave the theatre or shut the book without having made some kind of response to him and what he stands for. If our instinct is to hate anything that savours of dictatorship, we will look back with some approval to the

Tribunes who regard him as a hawk, preying on the people of Rome (Act I, Scene i, lines 73-6). Cassius, too, compares Caesar contemptuously with a god, fearing the prospect of his being crowned king (Act I, Scene ii, lines 116-32). Brutus himself is deeply troubled and, as he is a friend of Caesar, his decision to help in the conspiracy gives strong support to the idea that Caesar deserves to die (Act II, Scene i, line 10). Many other patricians in Rome feel the same way. Caesar himself is presented as arrogant in the very first scene and the harsh way he treats his wife because she is barren shows a lack of human feeling (Act I, Scene ii, lines 7-10). His deafness and tendency to epilepsy make him unattractive and, if these examples seem superficial, in more important matters he shows many qualities of a tyrant. When warned by his wife about the bad omens, he boasts,

> *Danger knows full well*
> *That Caesar is more dangerous than he:*
> *We are two lions littered in one day,*
> *And I the elder and more terrible.*

and in the last few moments of his life he not only spurns a petitioner like a cur out of his way, but indignantly asks those who want to press the matter further if they want to 'lift up Olympus', thus plainly suggesting his own god-like nature (Act III, Scene i, line 74).

Perhaps more serious is the charge that Caesar is ambitious. Casca says of him, when offered the crown that, *he was very loath to lay his fingers off it* (Act I, Scene ii, lines 242-3) and Brutus makes much of this point in his own funeral speech (Act III, Scene ii, line 27). Against this, we must note Brutus's free and obviously genuine admission that Caesar's 'affections' had never 'sway'd more than his reason' (Act II, Scene i, lines 20-1). Caesar's apparently calm acceptance of the prospect of death (Act II, Scene ii, lines 32-7) and his generous attitude towards the conspirators who call to escort him to the Senate (Act II, Scene ii, lines 109-23) reveal some of those qualities that had endeared him to his loyal supporters. In particular, there is the admiration that Antony felt for him and the intense determination that he showed in pursuing the conspirators to the end in order to avenge Caesar's death. More facts and details about Caesar can be found by reference to the Theme Index but enough has been said to show that the picture of Caesar presented to us is contradictory. This is surprising since he is, after all, the central figure in this drama, so the next step must be to discover why Shakespeare failed, deliberately or otherwise, to portray Caesar in a clear and consistent way.

It is possible that Shakespeare is doing his best for Brutus, who may be regarded as the central figure in the play, not Caesar. In other words, Caesar is made to appear generally bad and inconsistent so that Brutus can appear to be a more noble and clearly defined figure, a better person to be the true 'hero' of the play. If this is correct, the task is a difficult one, since the hero is a murderer of one of the most famous and successful men who have ever lived. Thus, perhaps Caesar is seen to be petty and contemptible (but not actually deserving of a violent death) so that sympathy can be drawn towards Brutus. But the murder is still seen as a brutal act yet, because it is done from the highest motives, a truly tragic situation is created for Brutus. Two of the more obvious qualities possessed by most of Shakespeare's heroes are (1) a certain nobility of character that makes them respected, if not admired, and (2) some fault or weakness that leads them, it seems almost inevitably, to their death. Both Caesar and Brutus seem fitted in these respects to be regarded as tragic heroes, and we must not dismiss too readily the belief that Shakespeare intended Caesar to be the dominant figure. But the essential nobility of Brutus's character is stressed time after time. When the conspiracy begins, it is to Brutus that all the conspirators turn, knowing that they are helpless without him. His value in this respect is expressed glowingly by Casca,

> O, he sits high in all the people's hearts
> And that which would appear offence in us
> His countenance, like richest alchemy
> Will change to virtue and to worthiness.
>
> (Act I, Scene iii, lines 157-60)

It is Brutus who sets a high moral tone for the whole conspiracy and who hates the apparent 'butchery' of Caesar, preferring to see it as a ritual sacrifice (Act II, Scene i, lines 166-74). Again, Brutus will not have Antony murdered together with Caesar for the same reasons of moral principle. In more personal ways, too, Brutus is an attractive character: he clearly loves his wife (Act II, Scene i, lines 288-91) and is concerned about the welfare of his troops and his servant-boy (Act IV, Scene iii, lines 248-65) and his stoical acceptance of the news of Portia's death (even making full allowance for the confusing nature of the text at this point) is something we cannot help admiring. But he does show an amazing self-righteousness, seen in the quarrel scene with Cassius (Act IV, Scene iii, lines 66-9) and in the parley before the final battle where he says to Octavius, who hopes he will not die at the hands of Brutus,

> *O, if thou wert the noblest of thy strain,*
> *Young man, thou couldst not die more honourably.*
> (Act V, Scene i, lines 59-60)

He is capable of overruling his friends and colleagues in a blunt and inconsiderate way and it seems at one point, when he needs money to pay his troops, that he is prepared to let Cassius soil his hands getting the money, and then to make use of it himself (Act IV, Scene iii, lines 75-7). He makes mistakes that probably ruin his cause, as when he refuses to allow Antony to be killed, and in allowing his troops to waste time plundering while Cassius is in difficulties (Act V, Scene iii, lines 5-8). Nevertheless, the purity of his motives, his almost complete lack of selfishness, the obvious admiration felt for him by all, even his enemies [note that it was Antony who said *This is the noblest Roman of them all* (Act V, Scene v, line 68)], and many other attractive qualities, are all strong reasons for regarding Brutus as at least the character who is most likely to reveal Shakespeare's general dramatic intention.

But firstly there are two other characters who must be considered. Both Cassius and Antony exhibit some of the complex and even contradictory qualities of Caesar and Brutus. Antony, a minor figure at first, suddenly bursts into the middle of the action immediately after the assassination. He is shown to be, as Cassius says, 'a shrewd contriver' (Act II, Scene i, line 158), a quality that is revealed in the scene where he appears to make friends with the conspirators. But this cunning springs from the passionate and genuine admiration he feels for Caesar. This violent loyalty and admiration is shown in his speech over the dead body of Caesar (Act III, Scene i, lines 255-76). His ardour and craftiness are understandable, knowing as we do the difficult and dangerous situation in which he finds himself, and we can probably bring ourselves to forgive him for that touch of ruthlessness that is necessary to overthrow a murderous conspiracy. But later we see an Antony who is cruel by nature, not through necessity, and the way in which he throws aside the lives of his own relatives with no pity or hesitation (Act IV, Scene i) shows us at once that we are not meant to look upon him simply as a just avenger of a cruel murder. For the rest of the play he is solely motivated by this burning determination to take revenge but his cruel methods, his contemptuous attitude to Lepidus (Act IV, Scene i, lines 12-15), and his squabbles with Octavius, weaken any feeling of sympathy he may have aroused through his devotion to his friend Caesar.

Cassius is usually regarded as the evil genius of the conspiracy and there is little doubt about his jealous and vindictive motives. As Caesar himself says of Cassius, with perfect insight, he can never be at heart's ease while beholding someone greater than himself (Act I, Scene ii, lines 209-210). In trying to win over Brutus, he produces petty examples of the weakness of Caesar that would only occur to a mean and spiteful man; he has no scruples about killing others, such as Antony, in order to ensure the success of the plot, nor about allowing bribery in order to obtain cash while on campaign. In this, his practical but immoral way of life is in contrast with Brutus's idealism, just as his shrewdness in knowing what is best in practical matters shows up Brutus's incompetence. He strongly disapproves of Antony being allowed to speak at Caesar's funeral and his fears are later proved to be perfectly justified; it seems likely that he was right to resist Brutus's plan to strike camp and march to Philippi for the final battle (Act IV, Scene iii, lines 198-204). But however clever Cassius may be, he seems doomed to failure from the start. Suicide is never far from his thoughts (Act I, Scene iii, lines 89-100 and Act III, Scene i, lines 20-2) and he is the one who panics when he fears that the conspiracy is discovered at the last moment. He always loses his arguments with Brutus and is particularly badly treated by his friend in the quarrel scene (Act IV, Scene iii). The quarrel itself is a bad omen for the two men and from then on Cassius is dogged by a sense of foreboding that in itself seems to eliminate any chance of success (Act V, Scene i, lines 77-89). Ironically, it is the shrewd, determined and practical Cassius who kills himself as a result of nothing more than a silly mistake of observation; the man who set himself up as a mirror for Brutus (Act I, Scene ii, lines 52-71) has faulty eyesight himself and we cannot help feeling that it is a lack of real 'vision' or insight in the vital matter of the aims and principles behind the conspiracy that indirectly brings about his downfall. Pity, rather than contempt, seems to be the most fitting reaction to Cassius's life and death.

The chief characters, then, are certainly vividly drawn, fascinating and strongly contrasted, but they contain conflicting elements and are not easy to sum up in simple terms. If we study lesser characters, such as Casca, similar qualities are shown. One obvious explanation of this may be that it is never easy to put people into categories, and Shakespeare's sense of realism persuaded him to present people as they really are rather than simplify them for dramatic neatness, as some lesser dramatists have done. But even if we make full allowance for this, the feeling of puzzling complexity or inconsistency persists. It seems that at this point the study of the play purely on the basis of character begins to break down.

Perhaps we should look upon the play as chiefly a political study. Here, though, we must beware of a danger. Today, there is a strong tide running in favour of democracy; the old beliefs in the value of an authoritarian structure of society are being seriously questioned and dictators are widely condemned. But it is very unlikely that these modern ideas about democratic government would have been held by many Elizabethans; certainly, there is a good deal of evidence in Shakespeare to show that an ordered hierarchy of society, from the king or queen downwards, was felt to be essential. Nevertheless, Shakespeare evidently knew and thought deeply about the immense problems caused by an all-powerful but incompetent or evil ruler, and the widespread belief that a monarch derived his authority from God only served to intensify the problem, since rebellion would involve not merely acting against the king but against God as well. Of course, Caesar was not an English monarch, but his status and reputation would probably persuade an Elizabethan audience to look upon him in much the same way as they would, for example, the king in one of Shakespeare's history plays. *Julius Caesar* may possibly be seen as a study of the consequences and dangers of trying to remedy the situation when a tyrant gains supreme power and wields it ruthlessly. The fact that the attempt, though initially successful in its aims, proves in the end to be a very costly failure (not simply in that the conspirators are hunted down and destroyed but because of the obvious triumph of the 'spirit' of Caesar), may indicate Shakespeare's own convictions about such attempts. If we assume that it does, we must not make the mistake of assuming that he was in favour of Caesar and all he stood for; it does not require a close reading of the play to know that the playwright could have made Caesar much more of a hero than he did. But we must also note that the play clearly is not actually centred upon questions of political power and the issues arising from it. For example, the effects of the conspiracy on the *private lives* of the characters are described at some length, as in the relationship between Brutus and Portia, and in the private thoughts and philosophies of most of the major characters. If questions of politics are the main issues, why do we see Brutus consider the question of murder in three agonizing soliloquies in Act Two, and almost wholly in a personal way, and then speak at length about the honourable nature of the act they are to perform? It seems that Shakespeare has more concern for individual people than the organization of the society in which they move. If this is true, then Shakespeare is really exploiting a certain political situation that existed at a certain time, to study people and their behaviour when influenced by such a situation. Are there any other clues in the drama that might lead us to a fuller appreciation?

The language of this play is not particularly 'poetical' by normal Shakespearian standards. In some of his greatest plays it is possible to detect complex patterns of images that reflect and emphasize the themes of the plays. Though *Julius Caesar* does have a number of recurring images, they do not show any particular pattern. There are a number of references to animals: for example, Casca is described as a 'cur' by Antony (Act V, Scene i, line 43), Caesar is seen by Antony as a hart pursued by hunters (Act III, Scene i, lines 208-11) and Brutus would prefer to be a dog and 'bay the moon' (Act IV, Scene iii, line 27) than accept bribes. The interesting point here is that the imagery shows human conduct in a debased form, thus emphasizing the mean or vicious behaviour that men are guilty of in the play. In contrast with this, the good qualities of people are expressed in terms of money or precious metals, as when Cassius speaks of his heart being 'dearer than Plutus' mine' (Act IV, Scene iii, line 101). Above all, there are numerous references to blood, either directly, or in figures of speech, which clearly have the effect of holding before the audience the ever-present effects of violence and the constant threat of violent death that hangs over most of the characters. It appears that the significant words and ideas are to be found expressed openly and explicitly in this play, rather than wrapped up in the poetry, and it is quite remarkable how frequently the thought of death occurs, together with its attendant dangers such as fate, chance and sickness. Of course, the central event is the death of Caesar, but Shakespeare does not just deal with the death of Caesar and its results in detail, he puts into the minds and mouths of many characters a wide-ranging consideration of death from every angle. See how Brutus not only debates within himself the question of Caesar's death at the beginning of Act II but elaborately describes the proposed murder as though it were a religious ceremony. In the following scene, Calphurnia's speech is full of descriptions of war, blood, graves yawning and men dying (Act II, Scene ii, lines 14-24) and Caesar himself philosophically resigns himself to the inevitability of his own end:

Of all the wonders that I yet have heard,
It seems to me most strange that men should fear,
Seeing that death, a necessary end,
Will come when it will come.

(Act II, Scene ii, lines 34-37)

Death constantly haunts almost all the characters and we are continually reminded of its sinister presence. The Tribunes who had removed the decorations from Caesar's statues and busts are, we are grimly told, 'put to silence' (Act I, Scene ii, line 287). Antony's prediction about the results of Caesar's death (Act III, Scene i, lines 255-76) is a gruesome prophecy, expressed in the most vivid terms, and his stripping of the corpse of Caesar before the crowd and the detailed description of the wounds given by each conspirator seem to be a part of the process, continuing throughout the play, of holding death up to view in all its horror. Quite often characters seem to invite their own deaths. We have seen already how Cassius does this. Both Brutus (Act III, Scene ii, lines 45-8) in his funeral oration, and Antony (Act III, Scene i, lines 152-64) in his speech to the conspirators, express their willingness to be killed by their own audiences. Both Brutus and Cassius, of course, are killed at their own command, but not before some long preliminaries in the case of Brutus. Portia, we learn, commits suicide (Act IV, Scene iii, lines 152-9). But the most vivid and frightening example of death is that of the unfortunate poet Cinna (Act III, Scene iii). Here, an innocent man is torn to pieces by the angry mob. Not only do the manner of his death and the injustice of it seem painful to us, but he seems drawn irresistibly towards his doom by some outside force which prompts him to do something he is not really inclined to do,

I have no will to wander forth of doors,
Yet something leads me forth (lines 3-4).

In much the same way, Caesar, though warned by the soothsayer and the bad omen of the sacrifice (Act II, Scene ii, lines 39-40) and in spite of his wife's pleas, not to mention the warning letter of Artemidorus, still insists upon going to the Senate. No doubt bravado and ambition for the crown play their part here, but we cannot avoid a feeling that some higher power is controlling his fate, compelling him to go to his death in spite of everything.

This power, called in the play fate, chance, 'the gods' (in a very general sense, and without much religious significance) or just referred to indirectly as the natural progress of a man towards his destiny, is a vital element. As mentioned in the introduction, superstitious fears do not affect us so much today as they used to in past history; but Shakespeare uses man's instinctive sense of powerful, and often hostile, forces weaving his destiny for him, to emphasize the atmosphere of uneasiness, fear, danger and ultimately death, which constantly pervades this play. Calphurnia is frightened by the storm and the extraordinary events in the streets of Rome and fears that they foreshadow danger for her husband (Act II, Scene ii, lines 13-26). Caesar himself, clearly disturbed, orders a sacrifice to be made as a kind of test of the omens and though his interpretation of the result is unusual and optimistic, it shows that Caesar entertains these superstitious feelings as much as anybody else. Casca is terrified by the storm; Cassius is delighted by it – but both regard it as very significant. Cassius is later filled with gloom by the sight of birds of prey hovering over his troops (Act V, Scene i, lines 88-9). In almost every case of supernatural influence, it is the fear of something terrible, with the smell of death about it, that causes the anxiety and doubt. In a similar way, illness is used to underline the prevailing sense of danger to life and limb. To give just one example, Ligarius (Act II, Scene i, lines 310-34), though he is meant to be physically unwell, suggests that he can 'discard' his sickness if there is work to be done for the benefit of Rome. In this case, the suggestion is that Rome itself is suffering from a kind of illness under the tyranny of Caesar.

The power of the Roman citizens as a mob was also referred to in the Introduction. Their violence and greed, their over-readiness to respond to a persuasive orator and their complete disregard for justice are all apparent from what they say and do. There seems no point in trying to defend them or plead that Shakespeare did not really intend them to be so irresponsible. Two points, however, may be made. Firstly, the obvious one that, through lack of opportunity, education, and because of a very low standard of living (by comparison with modern times) the ordinary people with whom Shakespeare was familiar in his own time could hardly be expected to have reached a reasonable level of social responsibility. Secondly, these citizens, for the most part, are treated as a mob or group acting together. They do not have individual personalities (with the exception, perhaps, of the cobbler in Act I, Scene i). There is plenty of evidence from other plays by Shakespeare that he had a deep understanding of and sympathy for ordinary people, as well as those of the more privileged classes. But more important is the question of the dramatic purpose of having the citizens in the play at all. It seems that they are the instrument for putting into effect the driving forces in the play that have already been referred to – the hatred of men, for example, and the power of fate. They thus represent an ideal and anonymous agent of danger and death and we should not pay too much attention to their social significance.

It would be foolish to attempt to summarize the 'meaning' of this play in any neat or simple way; Shakespeare makes such attempts seem peculiarly inadequate or silly, and in any case the best one does is to present only a small part of the truth. These notes attempt to direct your reading to a broadly-based view of *Julius Caesar*, not as an attempt to present a piece of history, nor even a commentary on tyranny and assassination. It certainly shows men and women under the intense pressures of stress and strife, and in particular the ultimate threat of death itself, and it seems that both the rule of tyranny and the attempt to overthrow that rule by violence have in common an element of futility with the prospect of violent death at the end of them. Shakespeare has employed common and basic human experiences – ambition, hatred, superstition, fear of fate, violence and the haunting dread and fascination of death, in his interpretation of history. The reader will obtain most value from this play if he accepts all these elements as a total experience in his reading and study.

THEME INDEX

The following lists of references are intended to assist those who study, or write on, particular aspects of the play. It is not suggested that these are the *only* themes with which Shakespeare deals, nor that the lists are comprehensive.

The atmosphere of anxiety and fear of the future that pervades the play can be seen from the following passages that are all in some way concerned with **superstitious fears and omens**:
I ii 1-25; I iii 1-78; II i 193-211; II ii 1-90; III i 1-2; IV iii 278-91; V i 77-92; V iii 23-5; V v 17-20.

Closely associated with these is the sense of **the power of Fate** and the importance of **accident** or **chance** in determining men's fortunes:
I ii 16-25; II ii 26-7; II iii; II iv 27-37; III i 1-12 and 99-101; III iii 1-4; V i 93-108; V iii 65-71.

These in turn lead to misfortune and finally **death**. The importance of death in the play has already been stressed and the following list of references is in itself impressive enough to show the significance of this theme:
I ii 87-90; I iii 89-102; II i 10-34 and 155-83; II ii 17-37 and 75-82; III i 20-2, 76-9, 99-117; 160-70, 196-211, 255-76; III ii 35-48 and 171-99; III iii; IV i 1-6; IV iii 93-107, 147-56 and 175-94; V v 5-51.

Men attempt to fortify themselves against these grim realities of life by means of **philosophy**. In particular, the contrasting philosophies of the Stoics and Epicureans can be seen in these passages:
I iii 91-9; II ii 26-37; V i 71-119; V v 21-5.

Shakespeare is fully aware of, and seems to admire, the peculiar virtues of **Romans** and the **glory of Rome** itself:
I ii 154-7, 173-6 and 198; I iii 57-8, 80-4 and 108-11; II i 47-55, 124-6 and 136-40; II ii 85-9; III i 106-19; III ii 20-48; IV iii 18-28 and 189-90; V i 111-13; V iii 98-102.

But he is equally aware of the cruelty of the mob and although the citizens appear in few scenes, their influence on the play is vital:
I i 1-76; III ii; III iii.

The language, and more especially the imagery of this play are not so significant as in some of Shakespeare's other works. However, the following themes occur:
Blood, butchery, dead bodies: II i 162-74; II ii 288-90, 76-90; III i 152-3, 205-11 and 266-76; III ii 176-80.
Animals: I iii 72-5 and 104-6; II i 14-15 and 32-4; II ii 46-7; III i 42-6, 205-10 and 274-6; IV i 22-7 and 29-34; IV iii 110-11.
Money and riches: I iii 157-60; IV iii 72-5 and 100-5.

The characters of the play used to be regarded as of supreme importance and, in fact, almost the sole reason for Shakespeare's plays being written at all. Modern criticism has established a better balance between the various elements in his plays, and provided that we do not lose a true sense of perspective, a study of the chief personalities in *Julius Caesar* can be very rewarding:
Julius Caesar: I i 70-77; I ii 1-25, 98-162 and 179-287; I iii 72-111; II i 10-34 and 193-211; II ii 1-127; II iii; III i 1-12, 31-77, 195-215 and 255-76; III ii 12-41 and 75-254; IV iii 278-91; V v 16-20.
Brutus: I ii 20-323; I iii 140-62; II i; II ii 110-29; III i 13-254; III ii 1-61; IV ii; IV iii; V i 21-70 and 93-126; V ii; V iii 91-110; V iv; V v.
Cassius: I ii 26-322; I iii 41-164; II i 86-223; III i 11-254; III ii 1-10; IV ii; IV iii 1-241; V i 21-122; V iii 1-50 and 60-106.
Antony: I ii 1-11; II i 155-91; II ii 52-6 and 116-17; III i 124-298; III ii 42-273; IV i; V i 1-66; V iv 16-32; V v 68-75.
Portia: II i 233-309; II iv; IV iii 147-68 and 183-97.
Calphurnia: I ii 1-9; II ii 1-107.

FURTHER READING

The literature on *Julius Caesar* is not only abundant but sometimes contradictory. This is no bad thing provided the student does not read simply to pick up useful critical ideas, but is prepared to think for himself.

The best reading on the relationship between Brutus and Cassius is in J. Dover-Wilson's introduction to his edition of the play (Cambridge University Press), if only because it presents a fairly traditional view, though strongly biased against Caesar. Thus, Brutus is seen as the tragic hero whose decision to murder Caesar is right, although it eventually proves disastrous for himself. An earlier but equally admiring view of Brutus was taken by M. W. McCallum in his *Shakespeare's Roman Plays* (Macmillan), though the style of this work may not be to the taste of modern readers. In contrast is J. Palmer's *Political and Comic Characters of Shakespeare* (Macmillan), especially Chapter I which is devoted to a study of Brutus but is not favourable to him. Harley Granville-Barker, in his *Prefaces to Shakespeare, Vol. II* (Batsford), was also dissatisfied with the heroic view of Brutus, but his general approach to the play is so enthusiastic, and he has such a sharp eye for the merits of the play as a stage drama, that he is well worth reading.

In the Signet Classic edition of the play (New English Library) there are long extracts from Plutarch for those who would like to study Shakespeare's source, and also an interesting comparison between past and present criticism. There is too a valuable essay on Caesar by R. A. Foakes. This may be supplemented by a reading of J. I. M. Stewart's *Character and Motive in Shakespeare*, Chapter III (Longmans), which suggests other ways of interpreting Caesar's character. There is a balanced and readable essay by W. Warde Fowler in his *Roman Essays and Interpretations* (Macmillan). The reader should not be put off by the other chapter headings but turn straight to the last one of all, headed 'The Tragic Element in Shakespeare's *Julius Caesar*' which deals with the playwright's handling of Plutarch, explaining why Cassius's character is not more fully developed. It must be remembered that Plutarch's view of Caesar is not a flattering one. A powerful case is made out for Caesar by T. S. Dorsch in his introduction to the Arden edition of the play (Methuen).

Turning to the language and the imagery, we are in deeper water. The original analysis was made by Caroline Spurgeon in *Shakespeare's Imagery* (Cambridge University Press) and the relevant parts of this may be referred to. Other useful works include M. Charney's *Shakespeare's Roman Plays* (Harvard) and the last chapter of A. Bonjour's *Structure of Julius Caesar* (Liverpool University Press).